About The Cover Design

"… [Yahweh] ordered the sea not to go beyond the borders he had set for it."

Proverbs 8:29a International Children's Bible

Front Cover Design: Photo by Arkin Si, Half Moon Bay, CA, USA, sea waves crashing on shore. Published on April 6, 2021. Free to use under the Unsplash License. Unsplash grants an irrevocable, nonexclusive, worldwide copyright license to download, copy, modify, distribute, perform, and use photos from Unsplash for free, including for commercial purposes, without permission from or attributing the photographer or Unsplash.

Back Cover Photo: Courtesy of Donna J. Barnett

FROM STUDENTS USING *GOD STILL SPEAKS*

God Still Speaks has given me confirmation that I am truly hearing God speak to me. It has admonished me to be still and obedient!

I love learning the root words and the context in which verses are written. I also enjoy the analogies and stories used to bring practical application.

Learning the unique ways that God has spoken to others has reminded me of the simple yet profound ways he has used to speak in my life. And it reminds me that seasons change and so will I.

Through *God Still Speaks* my connection with God has deepened. I was missing the many ways that God speaks to me.

God Still Speaks was the best study I've ever been in! Thank you for your transparency as a person! That allowed my walls to come down and really hear.

God Still Speaks has taught me that hearing God's voice is Spiritual not physical.

God Still Speaks has given me the freedom to acknowledge the voice of God in my personal walk and to lean into his love and guidance moment by moment.

God Still Speaks has given me greater understanding that not only do I need to be attentive to hear God speak, but that God "wants" to speak to me because he loves me.

Because of *God Still Speaks* I am actively listening … and hearing God's voice.

God Still Speaks is absolutely fantastic teaching. Awesome study.

I have always listened to God's voice and now I have learned to talk to him like if he is in front of me.

God Still Speaks puts into practice and explains how God speaks to me. I am learning to listen for His voice.

God Still Speaks gave me confidence in evaluating what voice I was hearing — His or someone else's! I *loved* this study.

God Still Speaks has confirmed for me that I can hear God speak!!

God Still Speaks has helped me to learn more about how God speaks, how to listen and recognize His voice, how to verify and confirm His direction.

God Still Speaks has encouraged me to be more attentive in my quiet time each morning.

Understanding the way to discern God's voice from Satan's has been tremendously helpful!

God Still Speaks has taught me it will be very difficult to hear God's voice unless there is silence and peace. It has taught me to obey the first time you hear His voice. The author made things very easy to understand.

GOD STILL SPEAKS

SPEAKS

THE KEY TO EFFECTIVE DISCIPLESHIP

DEBORAH ROEGER

Energion Publications
Gonzalez, Florida
2022

ISBN: 978-1-63199-795-2
eISBN: 978-1-63199-796-9
LCCN: 2022930798

Energion Publications
P. O. Box 841
Gonzalez, FL 32560
energion.com
pubs@energion.com

To Henry and Jody Neufeld

I am led to dedicate this book to you, the heart and soul of Energion Publications.

You are more than my publisher, you are true fellow Christ-followers. I recall with fondness the first time Derf and I prayed with you in your home. Little did we know how God would answer the prayers we prayed that night. I have watched over the last few months as you brought the *God Still Speaks* manuscript to life. I so appreciate your creativity and your partnership in laboring to advance God's Kingdom. Henry, I am immensely grateful for your expertise in biblical languages!

God knew what He was doing when He introduced us to you at Chumuckla Community Church in 2016. May He continue to be glorified by the work of your hands. With utmost love and respect,

Debbie Roeger

Disclaimer: In this Bible Study I will cite a wide variety of references. While I am comfortable citing the identified source for the specific point referenced, that does not mean that I have read, understand, or necessarily agree or disagree with that source on other points of theology or doctrine. Therefore, referencing various authors or Study Bibles is not intended to be a blanket endorsement of either.

Note: The presentation of Hebrew and Greek words I have used is designed to make those words easier to read and pronounce. As a result, some letters are not precisely represented.

ACKNOWLEDGMENTS

I am thoroughly convinced that no book moves from concept to completion without the efforts of a small army of support. I have had the most blessed privilege of having the selfless support of that army of co-laborers for which I am so very grateful.

The hesitation I have in writing this acknowledgement is that I'll inadvertently leave someone off the list. I prayerfully hope not to do so.

My first acknowledgment must go to the *Harmony Adult Sunday School Class* at Worthington Christian Church, Worthington, Ohio. My husband and I were a part of that class for many years. They were the first ones to ask us questions about hearing God's voice. The notes I prepared for them on that subject were written in the fall of 2009. Over the years, as I've learned and grown in my own ability to hear God's voice more clearly, those notes gave root to the Bible study, *God Still Speaks* and eventually they bore fruit in the form of this book. Thank you, *Harmony Class* for asking the question!

Thank you to family and friends who, when asked, willingly shared their own testimonies of hearing God's voice which has added a richness to the study beyond measure. Your testimonies have made the study practical and accessible to everyone.

I am grateful for the faithful prayers of so many of our prayer partners through all of the writing stages and the teaching of this study. I can't count how many times I knew the reason I was still standing was because you were on your knees praying!

I am thankful to our dear friend Joan Winchell who unselfishly gave her time to do a proofread of a finished draft. Joan's eye for details such as missing words, proper placement of commas, an occasional misspelling, simplifying run on sentences and adding comments regarding content clarification were invaluable!

My closest sister in Christ and most faithful prayer partner, Diane, deserves special mention. Seven years ago, God gave her the first hint that I would one day publish Bible studies I had written. She has remained unmoved from what she heard God say to her that day in prayer. I'm convinced she has invested countless hours in prayer over the matter since then.

I am thankful to Pastor Tom Sharron, Chumuckla Community Church, Pastor Dave Folkerts and Sr. Director Carol DeBlasis, both from Calvary Chapel Melbourne, for asking me to reconsider my reluctance to publish this study. They provided the nudge I needed to inquire of the Lord and then move forward.

Gratitude beyond what words can express goes to Derf my husband of 48+ years. He stands above the rest as my friend, my spiritual covering, my prayer partner, my encourager, my tech support (at all hours of the day and night) and the love of my life. While he did not write any of the words in this book, he has, in one way or another, invested himself in every one of them!

To God be the glory!

TABLE OF CONTENTS

CHAPTER 1

LAYING THE FOUNDATION

THIS STUDY IS written to help Christ-followers learn how to hear God's voice. As we will see in this Chapter, Scripture states in plain words that God speaks. Truth builds on truth as the Bible provides example after example of God speaking in words and ways people are able to hear and understand. Tragically, "although the voice of God runs through all experiences, most of us have diligently trained ourselves to ignore his voice and get on with the business of life."[1]

The fact that we serve a *living* God, that He invites us to have personal relationship with Him, that He speaks to us and that we can hear His voice makes those who follow Christ very unique. "Apart from God's personal involvement in our lives, our life experience will be no different than that of nonbelievers."[2] The real question is *not* whether God speaks, but whether we are willing to *listen*!

In recent years a variety of books and Bible studies have been released addressing the issue of hearing God's voice. When I look at the growing mound of evidence all around, it seems to me that we have entered a season on the Kingdom calendar in which God wants His Bride to *know* that He still speaks to us today. Not only that, He wants "*you*" to learn to hear His voice!

Because God is impartial and He does not play favorites, He is **not** choosing a few select super religious people to speak to.[3] God wants to speak to *all* of His creation — He wants each of us to know His plans. He wants us to come into agreement with His plan for our life so His will can be done on earth as it is in Heaven (Matthew 6:10). He wants us to know of His amazing love for us. He wants to be in relationship with us. He wants to reveal hidden mysteries to us that are relevant to the Kingdom Age in which we live (John 16:13). Why would a loving, creator God not want it to be so?

In her study, *Discerning the Voice of God*, Priscilla Shirer teaches: "It is contrary to the nature of God *not* to speak. He can and will speak to you. There are so many people who say they have a personal relationship with God, but they don't really think they can hear God's voice. How personal can that relationship be," Shirer asks, "if the two of you never communicate with each other? Do you really think that He loved you enough to *die* for you, but then doesn't love you enough to *talk* to you?"[4] The pattern of the Bible is that God related to people in order to share what was on His heart. In fact, according to Mark Batterson, God speaks in whispers so that we draw near to Him and hear His heart, not simply the words He is speaking.[5]

"Do you in the depths of your heart believe that God can and will talk to you?" "Do you really expect and anticipate that you can hear the divine voice of God?" Because if you don't, you will never spend time listening.[6] "The one who does not expect God to speak will discount every single time God does speak."[7]

A.W. Tozer explains, "Those who do not believe God speaks specifically will simply ignore or explain away all the times when God does communicate with them. However, those who spend each day in a profound awareness that God does speak are in a wonderful position to receive His words."[8] My own personal experience has been that the more attentive I am to God's voice, the more He speaks to me!

WHAT THE BIBLE SAYS ABOUT GOD'S VOICE

"The Bible is a collection of accounts that reveal God speaking to people to give them specific instructions they would never have known otherwise."⁹ In every case, the recipients recognized God's voice and comprehended what He was saying. In each of the Scripture quotes below I have placed in bold the portion of the text that relates to God's voice. Footnotes show the Hebrew or Greek word used in the original text along with an abbreviated meaning for that word.

For **God does speak**ᵃ— now one way, now another — though man may not perceive it. Job 33:14 NIV

I will stand upon my watch and affirm my foot upon the fortress and will watch to see **what he will say**ᵇ **in me** and what I shall answer to my question. Habakkuk 2:1 JUB

This particular version accurately translates the original Hebrew which reads: "to speak *in* me, not merely 'to' or 'with' me." The original language suggests that "the speaking of God to the prophets was an internal speaking and not one that was perceptible from without."¹⁰

My sheep **hear my voice**,ᶜ and I know them, and they follow me. John 10:27

But when He, the Spirit of truth, comes, He will guide you into all the truth; for He will not **speak**ᵈ on His own initiative, but whatever He hears, **He will speak**,ᵉ and He will **disclose**ᶠ **to you** what is to come. He will glorify Me, for He will take of Mine and will disclose it to you. John 16:13-14

Jesus had modeled for His disciples the intimacy He had in His own relationship with His Father. As surely as the disciples were

---

a   **Speak** (Hebrew word *dabar* "daw-bar") meaning to speak, declare, converse, command, promise, warn, threaten, sing; to speak with one another, talk

b   **Say** (Hebrew word *dabar* "daw-bar")

c   **Voice** (Greek word *phone* {fo-nay'}) meaning a sound, a tone; a voice; of the sound of uttered words; speech; of a language, tongue

d   **Speak**: (Greek word *laleo* {lal-eh'-o}) meaning to utter a voice or emit a sound; to speak; to use the tongue or the faculty of speech; articulate sounds; to talk; tell; to use words in order to declare one's mind and disclose one's thoughts; to speak

e   **Speak**: (Greek word *laleo* {lal-eh'-o})

f   **Declare**: (Greek word *anaggello* {an-ang-el'-lo}) which means to announce, make known, declare, tell of things done, to report, to set forth, to proclaim able to trust that Jesus spoke for the Father, they could trust that the Spirit Jesus would send (the Holy Spirit) will speak for Jesus. Since the Spirit would enable Christ-followers in John's day to hear whatever Jesus was still saying, the relationship between Jesus and His disciples could be as intimate as it had been when Jesus was in the world. All later generations of disciples, including you and I, are able to experience the *same* relationship Jesus had with His first disciples. In other words, "true disciples [of all generations] should learn to hear his voice just as accurately."[11]

> **You spoke**[a] by the Holy Spirit through the mouth of your servant, our father David: .... Acts 4:25 NIV

> The [Holy] **Spirit told**[b] Philip, "Go and join that chariot." Acts 8:29 HCSB

> While they were ministering to the Lord and fasting, **the Holy Spirit said**,[c]"Set apart for Me Barnabas and Saul for the work to which I have called them." Acts 13:2

> Then he said, 'The God of our fathers has appointed you to know His will, to see the Righteous One, and **to hear the sound of His voice**.[d] Act 22:14 HCSB

> And when they did not agree with one another, they began leaving after Paul had spoken one parting word, "**The Holy Spirit** rightly **spoke**[e] through Isaiah the prophet to your fathers, saying, ..." Acts 28:25-26a

> Long ago God **spoke** many times and in many ways to our ancestors through the prophets. Hebrews 1:1 NLT

In Hebrews 1:1 "spoke" is the Greek word *laleo*. Its use "contemplates the fact [of speech] rather than the substance of speech."[12] In Hebrews 1:1 *laleo* calls attention to the fact that God spoke to men, not the content of what He said.

---

a   **Spoke** (Greek word *epo* "ep'-o") means to speak, say
b   **Told** (Greek word *epo* "ep'-o")
c   **Said** (Greek word *epo* "ep'-o")
d   **Voice** (Greek word *phone* "fo-nay")
e   **Spoke** (Greek word *laleo* "lal-eh'-o")

The Holy Spirit also testifies to us about this. For after He **says:**[a] .... Hebrews 10:15 HCSB

NOTE: The portion I have placed in bold text in *all* of these verses has the regular meaning of communicating by voice in the original Hebrew or Greek text.

Other Scriptures which reveal God communicates:

Surely the Lord God does nothing Unless He **reveals His secret counsel** To His servants the prophets. Amos 3:7

For the devious are repulsive to the LORD; But **His private counsel** is with the upright [those with spiritual integrity and moral courage]. Proverbs 3:32 AMP (see also Psalm 25:14)

In Proverbs 3:32, the Hebrew word *sôd* {sode} translated as "counsel" refers to God's "most intimate, confidential talk."[13] We see this plainly in the NASB 1995 translation of Psalm 3:32b which reads, "But He is intimate with the upright."

The core meaning of *sôd* refers to what is private, intimate; secret counsel, especially a *confidential* plan, idea or confidence shared between friends and confidants.[14]

The righteous (upright) are those who do what God expects. They are the ones He confides in just as He confided in Abraham (Genesis 18:17).[15]

"Surely one reason some do not hear God speak specifically to them is because they don't really believe he will do so. Then, when God does speak, they refuse to acknowledge who it is."[16] Who will we choose to believe? Will we believe what God's Word teaches us about the truth that He speaks, or will we believe our doubt?

During his *Frequency Sermon Series* (based on the book he wrote, titled *Frequency*) Pastor Robert Morris recognizes that the Bible starts with God talking to Adam and Eve and it ends with God speaking to the Apostle John on the Isle of Patmos. His point

---

a   **Says** (Greek word *ereo* {er-eh'-o} meaning to call, say, speak of, tell (an alternate for *epo* in certain tenses)

is that God is talking all through the Bible. As a result, it is not logical to conclude that He doesn't speak today.

It would be very odd indeed to lead people into a *personal* relationship with Jesus and then say He doesn't speak to them. In fact, Dallas Willard concludes, "If God doesn't speak today, then the greatest disservice we could ever do to people is to tell them that they can have a *personal* relationship with God."[17]

This idea of divine-human relationship which is so familiar to followers of Christ today had its genesis back in the garden. When God created man He had wonderful, open communication planned for His children, but that was lost in the Garden of Eden!

> And they heard the sound of the LORD God walking in the garden in the cool of the day, and Adam and his wife hid themselves from the presence of the LORD God among the trees of the garden. Then the LORD God called to Adam and said to him, "Where are you?" So he said, "I heard Your voice in the garden, and I was afraid because I was naked; and I hid myself." Genesis 3:8-10 NKJV

Pastor Morris concludes that the narrative of Adam and Eve's sin in Genesis shows us that the reason people are afraid of God's voice is sin. Before sin, God's voice was welcomed. After sin, God's voice was feared. There is good news! The good news of the gospel is that God sent His Son to redeem us so that we can walk and talk with Him in the garden again! Jesus restored to us the ability to have relationship with God (in other words to be reconciled to Him) and to hear His voice. Our highest priority is to spend time with God. We were created to walk and talk with Him. Pastor Morris admonishes that biblical truths about God's voice and methods we can use to hear Him can be taught, but *no one* can develop *your* personal relationship with God for you. As we spend time with the Lord we recognize His voice.

CHAPTER 2

THE NORM NOT THE EXCEPTION

AUTHOR AND TEACHER John Eldredge, offers the following encouragement: "I realize that hearing God in such a direct manner might be a new experience for you. It certainly wasn't my experience for years. No shame in that. We're students, and we're all learning. Don't let your experience of God up to this point limit what you might enjoy with him in the coming years."[1]

IT IS NORMAL FOR CHRIST-FOLLOWERS TO HEAR GOD'S VOICE

When Jesus addressed Satan in the wilderness He made clear that hearing His Father's voice is a natural part of obedient discipleship.

> But Jesus told [Satan], "No! The Scriptures say, 'People do not live by bread alone, but by every word that comes from the mouth of God.'" Matthew 4:4 NLT

When God formed Adam and Eve and placed them in the Garden, He had created two living beings in His own image who were able to walk and talk with Him. They were His co-regents on earth. Their assignment from God was to rule His Kingdom on earth (Genesis 1:26).

When man substituted his own reasoning for God's perfect will, eating that which was forbidden for him to eat, the perfect fellowship he had with God in the Garden was broken. Jesus came to reconnect man to God; He was sent to reconcile the relationship that was broken by sin and re-open the direct access to God that had been lost (Colossians 1:20; 2 Corinthians 5:18-19; Romans 5:10-11).[2] At the death of Christ, the veil in the Temple was torn from top to bottom symbolizing the opening up of the way for renewed fellowship between the Creator and His creation (Matthew 27:50-51). Through the shed blood of Christ *every* disciple of Christ has the privilege of walking and talking with God once again.

As Jesus walked daily with His disciples they heard Him speak. He spoke to them the things He heard from His Father.[3] As we saw in the last Chapter, for centuries before that the Old Testament records God speaking through many different ways. Accordingly, Pastor Robert Morris concludes "it is crazy to think that [God] spoke [in various ways] for 4,000 years and then all of a sudden after the first century He got laryngitis."[4]

When Jesus was preparing to return to His Father, He told His disciples it would be an "advantage" to them that He was leaving them (John 16:7). "Advantage" is a translation of the Greek word *symphero* {soom-fer'-o} which in this context refers to uniting something together so as to be of even greater profit.[5] Jesus assured His disciples He would fulfill His promise and send the Holy Spirit who would be *in* them not just *with* them.

- ✓ He will teach you all things (John 14:26)
- ✓ He will remind you of everything I have said to you (John 14:26)
- ✓ He will testify about me (John 15:26)
- ✓ He will guide you into all truth (John 16:13)
- ✓ He will disclose to you what is to come (John 16:13)

Jesus reassured His disciples that the Holy Spirit would teach them, remind them, testify to them, guide them and disclose/reveal truth to them. That's exactly what we see the Holy Spirit doing in the early church.

Teach

> Galatians 1:15-17 — But when God, who had set me apart even from my mother's womb and called me through His grace, was pleased to reveal His Son in me so that I might preach Him among the Gentiles, I did not immediately consult with flesh and blood, nor did I go up to Jerusalem to those who were apostles before me; but I went away to Arabia, and returned once more to Damascus.

In his letter to the Galatians, Paul is suggesting that while he was in Arabia God Himself was His teacher through the Holy Spirit.

Remind

> John 2:22, bold added — So when [Jesus] was raised from the dead, His disciples **remembered** that He said this; and they believed the Scripture and the word which Jesus had spoken.

Testify

Acts 2:7 - After the Holy Spirit filled the apostles (Acts 2:4) on the day of Pentecost Peter preached to the crowd, testifying to the truth of Jesus whom they had crucified. Likewise, Stephen being full of the Holy Spirit (Acts 7:55) gave his defense to the high priest and his fellow Jews by testifying to the truth of Christ as revealed in the Scriptures.

Guide into truth

> Acts 13:9-10 — But Saul, who was also known as Paul, filled with the Holy Spirit, fixed his gaze on him,

and said, "You who are full of all deceit and fraud, you son of the devil, you enemy of all righteousness, will you not cease to make crooked the straight ways of the Lord?..."

I have heard the leading of Holy Spirit called, "God's GPS – God's Positioning System" which seems to capture the essence of His job description."[6]

Disclose

Book of Revelation - The entire book of Revelation discloses John's vision of the things to come.

Jack Deere, former professor at Dallas Theological Seminary, points out that some Christ-followers live all their lives without ever consciously experiencing a direct communication from the Father, the Son or the Holy Spirit. They read the Bible exclusively in terms of their own experience selectively filtering out the reality that God regularly communicated with His chosen servants. When they read the book of Acts, for example, they treat it as a historical document about the early beginning of the church rather than seeing the regular and recurring pattern of God's supernatural revelation. Every chapter of Acts, with the exception of one, "contains an example of, or a reference to, a supernatural revelatory communication from God to his servants."[7] Deere then proceeds to list at least one example from all 28 chapters with the exception of Acts 17.[8]

The book of Acts describes what it was like to experience God in the first century church. I agree whole heartedly with Deere's assessment that Luke's repeated stress on the creative ways in which the voice of God communicated so as to speak, warn, guide, deliver, inspire, comfort, predict and judge ought to make us very cautious about calling these experiences "abnormal" today. The sad reality is, if we're not regularly experiencing the Acts-type of communication with God, it is *our experience* which has been abnormal.[9] The good news is that the Holy Spirit stands ready to equip, empower and enable an entirely new experience — that of hearing and understanding God's voice!

According to Jesus teaching, reminding, testifying, guiding and revealing the future are all normal functions of the Holy Spirit. There is absolutely no place in the Bible that says His job description was confined to the first century church. Because every Christ-follower has the indwelling Holy Spirit that means *all* of these functions should be normal for *every* Christ-follower.

Priscilla Shirer points out that *all* of the Holy Spirit indwells every Christ-follower. "God does not give the Holy Spirit in installment plans; He doesn't place Him on lay away — a little bit now, a little bit later."[10] The issue is not whether you need more of the Holy Spirit to be an effective Christ-follower, but whether He needs more of you! As Shirer says, "That's because although you have all of Him, it is possible that He might not have all of you!"[11]

The Holy Spirit is not only our seal (our spiritual protection) He is also our guarantee that God will do what He says He will do (Ephesians 1:13-14). Because the *primary* way God guides Christ-followers today is by the Holy Spirit, it is vital we believe in the Holy Spirit not simply as a concept, but as a practical reality. Shirer quotes the preacher Dr. Stephen Olford who concluded: "The sin of the Old Testament is that they did not believe in God the Father; the sin of the New Testament is that they did not believe in Jesus Christ the Son and the sin of our generation is that we don't believe in the Holy Spirit."[12]

Our starting point then is to have confidence the Holy Spirit was given to each of us so we can hear God's voice. We must trust the testimony of the Bible that He enables us to receive direct guidance from God. Throughout this study I'll be adding present-day testimonies of God speaking in various ways. Jill provides our first testimony.

"Having been born in a Christ-centered home, communication with God was (and still is) the norm. Hearing God's voice, living in His Presence, is a lifestyle for me. It is hard to conceive there are Christians who are unaware the Holy Spirit speaks to His children. While I have never heard an audible external voice from the Holy Spirit, His promptings, His directives, His counsel, His corrections, etc., are ever present within me." ~ Jill (*not her real name*)

WHY DOES GOD WANT TO SPEAK TO US?

What we are primarily listening for when we listen for His voice is direction that we can obey immediately. His instruction might command us to "do" or "not do" something, to "think differently" or simply to "know" He is near.

"There are times that God speaks to you with the expectation that you will obey right away. My husband and I live in Florida where it can be quite hot and humid. One summer day after running a few errands I decided to stop at our community Welcome Center, which is on the water. It is one of my favorite spots to park, so I can talk and listen to God. That day I stopped and parked in the shade of a tree and turned the car off. God suddenly said "Go home!" Knowing His voice, I immediately turned on the car and went home, which is about 5 minutes from the park. As I walked into the house, I found my husband on the floor by the door slumped over ready to pass out. He had been working in the yard, done too much, become over heated and dehydrated. I was able to get his body temperature down and help him become re-hydrated. If I had not heard God's word to me, I might have gone home to a totally different situation. I am so grateful for my Heavenly Father speaking to me and that I obeyed immediately." ~ Pam

"One experience in particular comes to mind when asked to share concerning hearing the voice of God. One day, as I was cooking at home and waiting on someone to arrive, I was suddenly 'arrested' and led to intercede for that person. The time of intercession was intense and I perceived God was aborting the enemy's plan against that person that day although I did not know what it could possibly be. When the person arrived at home, I learned that on the way to the house, she got lost. She asked for directions from a gentleman and he instructed her to follow him and he would guide her to a certain point where she would be able to continue to her destination. So, she followed him for a while then suddenly, as though she snapped out a spell, she realized he was leading her away from her destination and into harm's way. She immediately turned around and eventually arrived at the house. The Holy Spirit's directive to intercede for her aborted the enemy's plan to harm one of God's children. Conversely, there have been times I have not heeded His voice and thus have paid a big price for it, in spirit, soul and body." ~ Jill (*not her real name*)

Our daughter, Kimberly, shared this experience with us which illustrates a different aspect of why God might speak to us:

"Yesterday we took the kids creek-exploring which was a great experience for them. It got really exciting when Abigail spotted a water snake right next to her! I had just had a thought about snakes in the water moments before and questioned Nathan if there were any poisonous water snakes to watch for — snakes hadn't crossed my mind until that point." ~ Kimberly

In each of these testimonies unbeknownst to the listener, God spoke to alert, prepare or warn of danger. With both Pam and Jill, Holy Spirit was warning of imminent danger requiring their immediate obedience. On the other hand, Holy Spirit had offered our daughter the *thought* of water snakes to put her on alert prompting her to question her husband about their safety. As she mentioned she had not been thinking of snakes whatsoever until moments before their 6-year spotted one in the water near to where she was standing. Our daughter was prepared exactly when she needed to be. Many people would dismiss these types of testimonies as coincidence; however, the truth is God loves to be involved in our daily life!

Not only does God want to share life with us, He has a destiny for us. The Bible tells us He has plans and thoughts directed at us!

'For I know the **plans** that I have for you,' declares the LORD …. Jeremiah 29:11a, bold added

"For My **thoughts** are not your **thoughts**, Nor are your ways My ways," declares the LORD. Isaiah 55:8, bold added

The simple truth of Scripture is that God wants to relate to us by speaking to us and guiding us into His plans and purposes — knowing, understanding and obeying His will is the key to effective discipleship.

Hearing God speak is vitally important to our discipleship. In fact, I believe it is the *key* to our discipleship! Jesus is not only our Savior, He is *Lord* of our life! We submit to Him and desire to know and do His will because we have made a commitment to follow Him. Bottom line, God's will for each of us is to conform us into the likeness of His Son. His voice is key to our transformation process. God will speak to shine a spotlight on our need. He will then describe that need and, if we give Him permission by coming into agreement with Him, He will also equip and empower us to meet that need. Throughout this study we will see a biblical pattern that *hearing* God equates with *obeying* Him and *knowing* God equates with *following* Him.[13]

God doesn't speak to indulge us; He speaks that we might be transformed by truth. Throughout the Bible when God speaks, He does so because He wants to reveal something about Himself, His plans and purposes or His ways. Henry Blackaby points out that those followers of Christ who have a track record of being mightily used by God are people who are determined to have God's guidance in *every* area of their lives.[14] Not all decisions/transitions we make in life are of the same magnitude. Some are as simple as a "page turn."[15] Some decisions/transitions are more like a new chapter. However, others are as significant as beginning to read an entirely new book. The "page turn" decisions are just as important to God as the major life decisions are. No matter how big or small the issue, God's Word assures us we *will* hear Him clearly when we ask Him for His wisdom with a heart that stands ready and willing to line up our life to His plan.[16] "The more we know His heart and ways, the more authority and responsibility He can trust us with."[17]

Andrew Murray, a South African writer, teacher and Christian pastor of the 1800's, summarized the first lessons in the school of hearing God's voice as follows: Set your heart to "receive what you do not comprehend, submit to what you cannot understand, accept and expect what to reason appears a mystery, believe what looks impossible, walk in a way which you know not."[18]

"Several years ago, I received a call from one of my friends at my church asking me to pray for her six-year-old niece who had just been rushed to the hospital in sickle cell crisis. Doctors were saying she would not make it through this one. She was unconscious and in ICU. I told my friend I would pray. I inquired of the Lord and was immediately impressed to call two specific partners on our church intercessory prayer team. I understood the three of us would be wielding the weapon of a triple braided cord in intercession. Upon the conclusion of our united prayer God told me to go to the hospital where the little girl was located. I told God I was not a family member and would not be permitted to visit her since she was in ICU. But the Lord said, 'You are to go to the hospital.' When I arrived at the hospital her grandmother was in the hall. I relayed to her why I was there. She summoned the nurse and requested I be given admission to see her granddaughter. I went to her bed side and she was not conscious. I did not know what to do but the Lord said, 'Lean down and sing Jesus Loves Me in her ear.' I did that and after the third time of singing it, her eyes opened, she lifted her head off the pillow and said she was hungry and asked for something to eat. God healed her totally. She is alive and well. She has been sickle-cell free for almost 30 years!" ~ Eva (not her real name)

"My husband had travelled to N.Y. and while there was admitted to a hospital due to a ruptured appendix. He called me and asked for prayer. The doctor had discovered a colony of bacteria on one of his organs and surgery was necessary to remove it in order to prevent it from being loosed into the bloodstream, which could prove fatal. I began to intercede for him. The strategy the Lord gave me was to base my intercession on the fact of His intercession, which I had just commemorated at the table of communion earlier that night at church. I know healing is His provision for us. When my praying was done, I told my husband that God has heard and has healed you. Tell your doctor to x-ray you again before the surgery tomorrow. He will see the problem is gone. Although my husband said OK, I was not sure he was alert enough to follow through by talking with the doctor. I was able to speak with his doctor later that night and gave the information directly to him. The doctor promised me he would do as I asked. Later that morning, I received a call from my husband and I spoke to both he and the doctor. They said no bacteria was present anywhere and he gave my husband the two x-rays as proof." ~ Eva (not her real name)

We set our hearts on hearing God's voice not simply for the purpose of receiving instruction; there is a much larger, more amplified reason for wanting to hear His voice. It is the way we truly come to know Him!

"Jesus had come to know his Father the way a son does; not by studying books about him, but by living in his presence, listening for his voice, and learning from him as an apprentice does from a master, by watching and imitating."[19] Jesus then acted "as a window"[20] for others to see the Father as He saw Him. Through Jesus, through His words and His actions, people came to know the Father. He set a pattern for His first century disciples and that pattern has never changed. Every disciple in every century is called to come to know the Father the way Jesus did, then to act as a window which will permit others to see the Father as you see Him.

In our western culture we have been taught that the Holy Spirit is our teacher so we think God will speak to our intellect, provide some explanation and by that we will then have knowledge. But God's way is just the opposite of this. "*We must live and experience truth in order to know it....* True discipleship consists in *first* following and *then* knowing the Lord."[21] This is a foundational biblical principle.

Andrew Murray provides a very simple description of the two ways in which we can *know* something.[22]

> The one is in the mind by thought or idea—I know about a thing. The other is by living—I know by experience. An intelligent blind man may know all that science

teaches about the light by having books read to him. A child who has [experienced light but who has] never thought what light is knows more about light than the blind scholar. The scholar knows all about it by thinking. The child knows it in reality by seeing and enjoying it.

God's revelations are designed to bring you into an increasingly deeper and profound love relationship with Him.[23] *All* that He says is designed to draw us into a deeper more intimate love relationship. He speaks and acts so we can know Him by experience. Knowledge based on personal experience is the biblical pattern. For example: let's consider some key passages which illustrate this well documented pattern that experience leads to knowledge:

"… The Egyptians shall **know** that I am the LORD, when I stretch out My hand on Egypt and bring out the sons of Israel from their midst." Exodus 7:5

This is what the LORD says: "By this you shall **know** that I am the LORD: behold, I will strike the water that is in the Nile with the staff that is in my hand, and it will be turned into blood…." Exodus 7:17

But on that day I will set apart the land of Goshen, where My people are living, so that no swarms of flies will be there, in order that you may **know** that I, the LORD, am in the midst of the land. Exodus 8:22

Moses said to him, "As soon as I go out of the city, I will spread out my hands to the LORD; the thunder will cease and there will be hail no longer, so that you may **know** that the earth is the LORD's …." Exodus 9:29

Then the LORD said to Moses, "Go to Pharaoh, for I have hardened his heart and the heart of his servants, that I may perform these signs of Mine among them … that you may **know** that I am the LORD." Exodus 10:1-2

"… Thus I will harden Pharaoh's heart, and he will chase after [Israel]; and I will be honored through Pha-

raoh and all his army, and the Egyptians will **know** that
I am the LORD...." Exodus 14:4

Then the LORD said to Moses, "Behold, I will rain
bread from heaven for you; and the people shall go out
and gather a day's portion every day ...." So Moses and
Aaron said to all the sons of Israel, "At evening you will
know that the LORD has brought you out of the land of
Egypt; ...." Exodus 16:4-6

"I have heard the grumblings of the sons of Israel;
speak to them, saying, 'At twilight you shall eat meat, and
in the morning you shall be filled with bread; and you
shall **know** that I am the LORD your God.'" Exodus 16:12

I will consecrate the tent of meeting and the altar;
I will also consecrate Aaron and his sons to minister as
priests to Me. I will dwell among the sons of Israel and
will be their God. They shall **know** that I am the LORD
their God.... Exodus 29:44-46

Now the LORD said to Joshua, "This day I will begin
to exalt you in the sight of all Israel, that they may **know**
that ... I will be with you...." Joshua 3:7

... Elijah the prophet came near and said, "O LORD,
the God ... today let it be known that You are God in
Israel and that I am Your servant and I have done all these
things at Your word. Answer me ... that this people may
know that You, O LORD, are God ...." 1 Kings 18:36-37

Thus I will strengthen the arms of the king of Babylon, but the arms of Pharaoh will fall. Then they will
know that I am the LORD, when I put My sword into the
hand of the king of Babylon and he stretches it out with
it against the land of Egypt. Ezekiel 30:25

The secret [counsel; Hebrew *sôd*] of the LORD is for
those who fear Him, And He will make them know His
covenant. Psalm 25:14 (You may recall that we have learned
that the Hebrew word *sôd* {sode} translated in Psalm 25:14 as
"secret" refers to God's "most intimate, confidential talk.")[24]

In each of these Scriptures the word "**know**," highlighted in bold text is a translation of the Hebrew word *yada`* which refers to an intimate knowledge based on experience. God performs some action and that action is designed and aimed at gaining experiential knowledge about Him. Knowledge which is gained by experience allows us to have absolute confidence (assurance) of the truth.[25] Therefore, it should not be surprising to us that God's pattern for His disciples is **Listen • Do • Know**.

In the western culture we hear something and we believe by merely *hearing it* that we know it and then because we know it we may do it (act on it). Scripture reveals a very different pattern. Biblically we see that God asks us to listen to what He says and even as we listen we are to have complete and immediate obedience parked firmly in our heart. Our mindset as we listen should be: "whatever He says is what I'll do." After we hear what He says, we are to *do* what He said to do. By *doing* it we come to *know* Him by experience.

The "new" covenant, which is the basis of our relationship with God today, was announced by both Jeremiah and Ezekiel who were prophets at the same time in Israel's history.

> Moreover, I will give you a new heart and put a new spirit within you; and I will remove the heart of stone from your flesh and give you a heart of flesh. I will put My Spirit within you and cause you to walk in My statutes, and you will be careful to observe My ordinances. Ezekiel 36:26-27

> "Behold, days are coming," declares the Lord, "when I will make a new covenant with the house of Israel and the house of Judah, not like the covenant which I made with their fathers in the day I took them by the hand to bring them out of the land of Egypt, My covenant which they broke, although I was a husband to them," declares the Lord. "But this is the covenant which I will make with the house of Israel after those days," declares

the LORD, "I will put My law within them and on their heart I will write it; and I will be their God, and they shall be My people. They will not teach again, each man his neighbor and each man his brother, saying, 'Know the LORD,' for they will all know Me, from the least of them to the greatest of them," declares the LORD, "for I will forgive their iniquity, and their sin I will remember no more." Jeremiah 31:31-34

Ezekiel prophesied a unique and specific type of heart which would be given as an end-times gift from God enabling and empowering obedience.[26] Both Jeremiah and Solomon linked "knowing" [*yada'*] God with God's Torah (His teachings/instruction/commandments) being "written on the heart."[27] By the repeat process of **Listen • Do • Know** we assimilate God's Torah as a way of life within our governing center (i.e. our heart) which changes and develops our character so that we keep those teachings/instruction/commandments from within! Plain and simple — that's true discipleship and it is the heart of the new covenant.

Just as we can never know God except by our experience; we will never *know* God's voice by simply acquiring facts about the subject of hearing God's voice. It is sort of like learning to ride a bicycle — you can look at photos of bikes, read all about them, even memorize important facts about how they are made; but you will never know how to ride a bike without committing yourself to do it. You must take risks and practice. God has intentionally designed the learning process whereby we come to know Him and His voice to require committing ourselves to the process, taking risks and practicing.

CHAPTER 3

COMMON WAYS GOD SPEAKS

I N THIS CHAPTER we will begin to zoom in on specific ways God can choose to speak to us. The study covers twelve of the most common ways Christ-followers experience God's voice. We will make the point more than once, however, that the common methods we will consider are in no way intended to be the outer limit of God's vocal range. He is a creative God and He can choose to speak in unimaginable ways that serve His purpose and highlight that He is a God without limit! This Chapter will highlight the first three ways, Chapter 4 will then focus on the remaining nine methods.

Before we begin to unpack specific ways in which God speaks, we need to know Rule #1 — there is no formula! When God knits each person together in their mother's womb (Psalm 139:13) He makes each one unique and individual. He knows exactly how He created us and that includes the knowledge of how we were created to uniquely hear His voice. As a result, He knows how to speak to us not just corporately, but distinctively and individually. The way He speaks to another person may not be the way He chooses to speak to you. God alone chooses "how" He speaks. Beware of comparison with how someone else hears God — comparing is a tool the enemy uses in order to cause envy and/or discouragement.

Among the most common ways to hear what God has to say
to you are:

- ✓ His audible voice
- ✓ His written Word
- ✓ an inner voice
- ✓ dreams and visions
- ✓ other people (either wise counsel we seek or generally)
- ✓ music
- ✓ His creation
- ✓ the sense of peace in our hearts
- ✓ miracles
- ✓ repetition
- ✓ silence
- ✓ circumstances (including unpleasant circumstances)

This is not intended to be a comprehensive, all-inclusive list.
God is creative and can find ways to speak to us that are unique
and creative. Two testimonies will illustrate this truth perfectly for
us. The first is from Nathan, our son-in-law and the second from
our daughter Kimberly.

God can use a fortune cookie! "When we went to purchase our home the max we could afford was $65,000
— the house we were interested in was listed for
$84,000. I asked God what to submit as an offer and
heard clearly that I was to offer $65,000. The owner respond-
ed with a counter of $72,000. So, I prayed about how to
respond and heard God say I was to counter with my original
offer of $65,000. That struck me as really strange because it
isn't how negotiation is done! The thought crossed my mind
that maybe I needed to 're-educate God' on how these things
work and at least offer $66,000. The last place I might have
expected God would make His instruction clear to me was in
a fortune cookie — but after eating dinner I split open my
fortune cookie and read this message: '*Listen attentively and in
the coming days you'll come out ahead.*' As odd as it sounds, I

knew this was God's counsel to me. So, I made the counter offer of $65,000 and waited — it was accepted!" ~ Nathan

God can use a quarter! "My husband was graduating from Vet School in Ohio and there was much anticipation about where God would lead us for his first job. When Nathan told me that he heard the job offer would be in Kansas (about 1100 miles away), I definitely wanted confirmation and asked God to provide that to me. After praying that prayer, I was pulling together quarters to do laundry. One particular quarter caught my attention. As I looked closer at it, I thought 'I've never seen that particular quarter before, I wonder which state it is from?' I turned it over and almost laughed to myself when written on the back of that quarter was 'Kansas.'" ~ Kimberly

It bears repeating that in His Sovereignty God alone chooses not only *when* but also *how* He will speak to us.

Many in the church today likely recognize some of the methods I listed above, but unfortunately too many of us are prone to quickly dismiss those we are least familiar with. The experience we have personally had with God becomes the outer limit for the way in which we believe He can and will speak (not only to us, but to anyone else as well). I believe this is a form of unbelief, it limits God and "puts Him in a box" expecting Him to do things according to our limited understanding.

As we have noted, God created us as individuals and He speaks uniquely and personally to us. In fact, He "is big enough to speak as many languages as there are people."[1] He does it in a way that pleases Him. As you pursue an intimate love relationship with God, you will come to recognize His voice and you will grow in your ability to know both *when* and *what* He is uniquely and personally communicating to you.

Jack Deere reasons, "Apparently, [God] enjoys speaking in a variety of ways and expects us to listen to any way in which he chooses to communicate. The more of his ways we *can* hear, the more we *will* hear."[2] I whole heartedly agree. Let's zoom in for a

closer look at these ways in which God still speaks. We will begin
our review with His audible voice.

SPEAKING AUDIBLY

God's voice can take many forms. Of course, the most explicit and authoritative ways He speaks is audibly. While I have never
personally heard the audible voice of God myself, I know others
who have. This next testimony is from my husband, Derf.

"Around my 14th birthday I recall crying out to the
Lord one night in bed, 'Lord why am I here, what's my
purpose, why was I born to *these* parents?' My aging
parents had lost several friends over the past few years; they
had other friends fighting cancer and I really wanted to help. I
wanted to help relieve pain and suffering. Much to my surprise,
God visited me that night I cried out and I heard what seemed
to me to be His audible voice. It was the first time I had heard
God speak in any fashion; but there was no mistake in my mind
that it was God speaking! The voice seemed so 'loud' to me
that I thought for sure my mom, who was a very light sleeper,
would be coming into my room to tell me to 'turn that radio
off!' In retrospect I wish I would have written down exactly what
God said that night. As I recall, He said 'you will find/discover
a power/energy to free all peoples.' I was ecstatic and said to
myself, 'Yes, fame and fortune!' The Lord immediately spoke
again and simply said that would not be the case; however, I
was still full of positive determination to pursue this worth-
while direction for my life." ~ Derf

My husband had no doubt whatsoever that the voice he heard
was God's voice. In fact, to his ears the voice that spoke to him was
so "audible" he thought his mom would soon be at his bedroom
door to tell him to turn the volume down on the *radio* he was listening to! What he heard that day gave direction to his life.

"My son was a starter on his middle school basketball
team. One day he returned home from practice complaining of a slight pain and walking with a slight limp.

He informed me he was unable to fully participate in basketball practice. His Dad and I decided to see how he fared overnight and, if not significantly better in the morning, we would take him to the doctor. That night, I was awaked at 1:58 a.m. by the audible voice of the Lord saying, 'Eva, wake up and pray.' As I tumbled out of bed unto the floor to get on my knees, I asked the Lord what He wanted me to pray for. He began to show me a list of names that just rolled down in front of me like movie credits at the end of a movie. Some of the names I knew, most of them I did not know. As I was concluding the prayer, the Lord asked, 'What about Aaron?' I said, 'Oh yes, I forgot. Would you heal Aaron's knee, Lord?' He said, 'Get up and go into His room and place your hand on the injured knee.' I said, 'Lord, I do not remember which knee.' The Lord said, 'the right one.' And I said, 'Lord, do You mind if I put one hand on each knee to make sure I am hearing you correctly insuring I get the right one?' He said, 'OK. That's fine.' So, I did exactly that. The hand that was on Aaron's right knee experienced an intense, super warm, but soothing heat sensation throughout my hand penetrating into his knee. When the sensation subsided, after several minutes, I went back to bed. The following day, when Aaron got home from school, he reported that we would not need to take him to the doctor because he was fine. He stated his right knee was fine and he was able to fully participate at basketball practice. I related to him the activity that took place while he slept the night before. He exclaimed, 'God actually healed my knee.'" ~ Eva (not her real name)

"I was 20 and had been working with Pitney-Bowes about 3 months. My boss knew I was active in church and one week I asked him if I could get off a little early on Friday. I was planning to attend a youth/college retreat which had dinner planned for 5:00. I needed time to get home, shower and make the drive. I made it home about 3:30, took a quick shower, dressed and headed out the door for Wilmer UMC. I got in my 68 Pontiac Tempest, backed up and then headed toward the street down our 100' gravel driveway. This being a newer car, I was not accustomed at that time to using my seat belt. However, about half way down the drive I heard an audible voice say, "Fasten your seat belt." I thought what? I heard it again but the voice was stronger this time, "FASTEN YOUR SEAT BELT." The voice I heard was strong and firm, loaded with authority. I could not resist its "command" so I stopped momentarily and fastened my seat belt then proceeded to the street. I was three driveways from Moffet Road, Hwy 98, and would be making a left turn. As I got about 100 foot from the stop sign, a speeding car came around the corner from the left taking both lanes. I slammed on the brakes and came to a stop. It just missed hitting me by about 10', but I knew in that moment I had just "dodged a bullet so to speak." It was a 20 minute drive on 98 to the church and I was under conviction the whole way. I immediately entered the sanctuary, knelt at the altar, poured my heart out to God and dedicated my life to Him. I don't remember anything else of that whole weekend, but still get cold chills when I just think about driving up my driveway. I know for sure had I not taken that 3-5 second pause to obey the voice I heard, the car would have hit me head-on or slammed into my driver's door, badly injuring me if not killing me on the spot." ~ Keith

In each testimony the listener heard what they understood to be a "self-authenticating"[3] voice providing them with instruction. They didn't need anyone to explain the voice they heard, they *knew* it was God.

While God can speak audibly "that is a thin slice of His vocal range ... His ability to speak is not limited to our ability to hear audibly."[4] God also speaks through a wide variety of other ways. Mark Batterson collectively refers to these other methods as "the inaudible yet unmistakable voice of God."[5] Although in these cases God's voice bypasses our ear gate we can rightfully use the word "speak" to describe the communication God has with us. The definition of "speak" is most commonly thought of as: "to utter words or articulate sounds with the ordinary voice." However, the common usage definition also includes "to communicate ... or disclose by *any means*."[6]

SPEAKING THROUGH HIS WRITTEN WORD

"God speaks to give *application* of his Word to the specific circumstances in your life."[7]

It was the morning of December 24, Derf and I were visiting our daughter and her family in Kansas to celebrate Christmas with them. The children were so excited that THIS year Grandma and Grandpa would be able to see their Christmas play at church in person rather than through a video their mom would usually take and send to us. Derf and I are always excited about any opportunity to worship with our children and grandchildren, but especially THIS particular morning. However, I woke up early that morning with a case of stomach flu so intense I was barely able to stand up. I could not believe it! I had not had flu in many, many years and figured I must have picked it up during the 3 days of travel to their home. I began to pray and ask the Lord for a miracle. I opened His Word and began to drink in His truth. I desperately wanted to be in church with my family that morning. When my daughter learned I had the flu, she suggested that the children pray for me. I sat there with great expectation and earnest hope as our son-in-law, our daughter and our 4 grandchildren prayed. The very moment that prayer was finished, my youngest grandchild, Abigail, 4 years old, sneezed one time. The Holy Spirit immediately reminded me of the story of Elisha who restored life to the Shunammite woman's son (2 Kings 4). When life returned to the boy's body he sneezed 7 times and then opened his eyes (2 Kings 4:35). As strange as it sounds, because that Scripture came to mind at the time Abigail sneezed I knew with certainty that God was telling me He had answered our prayers. I announced to my family, that Abigail's sneeze was God's assurance the flu had left not only me but their household. And sure enough, within the next 30 minutes I was ready for church feeling completely fine and the flu did not return! It is so important to be familiar with God's Word so that we can rightly hear His voice when He speaks to us.

"When the Lord began speaking to us about having our first child I was curious to know whether we were going to have a boy or girl. God kept bringing to mind the biblical story of Hannah and Samuel — but that still meant our baby could be either a boy or a girl. However, when my husband told me that God had given him the name 'Hannah Anna' for the baby, we had very clear confirmation that this baby would be our first daughter." ~ Kimberly

In a season when my husband and I were teaching a weekly Adult Sunday School class, one of the class members shared a story that illustrates how God can use His word when it has been stored in our heart. This man had a gift for memorization and had committed to memory much of the book of Psalms. He was an avid hunter and eager to get out on the first day of hunting season one year. He explained that he was in a transition season of life and would have greatly benefited from the food a successful hunt would provide. As he described that day he said it seemed to him as if *everything* went wrong, including the fact that he got lost in the woods. By the time he had found his way back to his tree stand he was tired and angry. He sat there frustrated and decided to rehearse Scripture he had been memorizing. In the midst of his frustration, there were two questions running through his mind: "God, am I in the right place in my life?" and "Is my faith going to be rewarded?" He began reciting from memory these words of Psalm 42: "As the deer pants for streams of water, so my soul pants for you, my God ..." At that very moment he looked up and the largest buck he had ever seen was standing by the creek! Bagging a deer was no longer his goal. Instead he sat in awe that although God had not spoken a single word to him, he knew with certainty God had provided the answer to his searching questions. He now felt certain God could handle his present circumstances.

What this man had done was refocus his thoughts using Scripture he had memorized. As long as he was rehearsing his failures, he was stuck in those debilitating thoughts. As soon as he began to recite Scripture from memory, his attention turned from his current circumstances to God. While he focused on God, God chose to show up in the midst of those circumstances in a way that he knew without doubt was unmistakably Him. Because he had taken the time to memorize Psalm 42 he could recall God's Word and recite it while sitting in a tree stand in the middle of the woods!

The Continual, Habitual Practice of Reading God's Written Word, the Bible, Is a Must (this is non-negotiable!)

As a general rule, "Anyone who wants to hear God's voice on a regular basis will have to become intimately acquainted with the written Word of God."[8] As you increase the time you spend in God's word you increase your opportunities to hear God speak.

Anne Graham Lotz shares an analogy God gave her which highlights the various ways we often approach the Bible. He used the birds she was watching at the beach as examples.[9]

> Anne, the Bible is like the ocean. And the people who read My Word are very much like [the] birds [you see at the ocean]. Some will dance around the Scriptures [like the sand pipers dance around the waves on the beach], not really wanting to step in and get their feet wet in Bible study. [They] are satisfied to just listen to their preacher or Bible teacher tell them what the Bible says.
>
> Others will read their Bibles, just skimming the surface for facts and information [like the skimmers who fly over the surface of the water]. Some will get in knee-deep [like seagulls who stand in the water up to their knees], reading the Bible each day with a devotional or commentary close by for reference. And then there are some like the pelicans, who dive in over their heads, going deep in Bible study, applying and living out what they learn. Which bird are you most like?

Reading the Bible should not be merely an academic exercise separated from life. We need to become like pelicans, to listen for God's heart and His voice as we read; we need to submit our lives to be transformed by Scripture.[10] Scholar Craig Keener advises:[11]

> In our Western culture we're addicted to shortcuts; we want everything instant. So we settle for verses out of context because somebody we look up to quotes them. We'll never get at the heart of the biblical texts without paying attention to how God inspired them originally— and He inspired them in their literary context, and also in addressing particular situations. Hearing how God addressed people in their concrete situations helps us when the Spirit leads us to apply the same principles to our different yet equally concrete situations today.

It is important to catch what Keener is advising here — we don't just *read* God's Word — we certainly can't be safe lifting a word or a sentence or even a paragraph out of context in order to make it fit any situation we desire. God's Word is not like a fast food drive through window with the promise of having it served up *your way*. To truly know what God is saying in His Word requires searching out the matter — working to understand who God was speaking to, the context in which He was speaking and what specific situation was He addressing when He spoke. His principles are timeless. When we make these careful observations *then* we can know how to apply His Word to our lives.

Anne Graham Lotz teaches participants in her study, *Expecting to See Jesus*, a 5-step process for reading, discerning and applying God's Word to their lives.[12] She stresses that the overall goal of this process is to listen to God's voice whenever you read your Bible. The steps she lists are in essence: 1) read a passage; 2) list the significant facts of that Scripture; 3) look for the spiritual lessons in that text; 4) identity what God is saying *to you* through this passage and 5) decide how will *you* apply it.

In his 2016 book, *Chase the Lion*, Mark Batterson wrote: "How do you discern the voice of God? It starts with the Word of God. If you want to get a word *from* God, get into the Word *of* God. That's how you learn to discern the voice of God. After all, it's the Spirit of God who inspired the Word of God. And when the Spirit of God quickens the Word of God, it's like hearing the voice of God in Dolby surround sound."[13]

Batterson's counsel lines up perfectly with my own experiences and especially with something God spoke to me while I was journaling in 2014: "My Word is not only Truth, it is Spirit. The more you drink in of the Spirit of my Word, the clearer you will recognize my Spirit in operation in you and all around you. It is like putting food into the body or putting gas in your car. You know it is needed, but you do not *see* how it works. You only know it does [work] and you benefit from it. And so, it is when you come morning by morning to meet with Me in My Word."[14]

Because the Spirit of God is alive and active in and through the Word of God (Hebrews 4:12) it just makes good sense that the more time we spend in God's written Word the easier it is to discern when God's Spirit is speaking to us. It is like a friend who calls you frequently. You get to the point where you have experienced that particular voice on the phone so often that you know the voice as soon as they say, "hello." There is no need for them to introduce themselves by name.

It is the Spirit of God who speaks to us and He speaks the mind of God.[15] "Scripture reading is meant to aid in the process of 'forming Christ within us.'"[16] In fact, Jack Deere rightly cautions, "If our Bible knowledge grows faster than our love, we will become arrogant."[17]

"So how do you read your Bible? Do you read it to increase your knowledge of the facts and information only? Or do you read it listening expectantly for God to speak to you, then talk to Him about what He said? ... God still speaks to us personally through His Word ... but we need to learn to listen to His voice. One way to listen is to pray before you read your Bible. Talk to God about what's on your heart and mind. Then open His Word and 'listen' with your eyes on the page. He may not speak to you every time you read it, but He will speak."[18]

"At 32 years of age and a brand new believer in God's word, I was in secular counseling for depression and marital distress. My counselor began to tell me that I could seek a divorce and shared how well she was doing after hers. She was strong and I was weak so I began to consider the idea. But I was learning how to pray and learning to read and believe in the truth of Scripture. God led me to two verses: Malachi 2:16a: "For I hate divorce, says the Lord." And Psalm 119:24: "Thy testimonies are my delight; they are my counselors." I quit counseling and began investing in Christian Bible Studies instead of seeking secular counseling and a divorce. My husband and I have been married for 52 years now. God's powerful word changed my thinking and saved our marriage!" ~ Samantha (not her real name)

Priscilla Shirer admonishes, "there ought to be a time in our relationship with Jesus where 'hand me down revelation' about God, spoon fed to us by someone else is no longer enough!"[19] While God's written Word contains wonderful revelation that should impact our lives, we all face life decisions which require a *personal* and *specific* Word from God. Shirer continues, "we can look at others who seem to receive fresh revelation from God and think they have some special type of relationship with God that is not available to us. But nothing could be further from the truth! The very same Holy Spirit that lives in them, lives on the inside of every Believer. God does not play favorites. In fact, *you* are His favorite! We each have the privilege of hearing the voice of God."[20]

"Sometimes through reading Scripture and being in God's Word, I will come to a passage, and I just have to stop and ponder or meditate, and ask "Lord, what do You want me to know in this moment?" How will Your Word draw me closer to You today, as I trust You and rely on You for my provision today? He always shows up, sometimes immediately and other times a day or two or a week later. BUT He ALWAYS shows up." ~ Colleen

In his book, *Surprised By The Voice of God*, Jack Deere concludes: "One of the reasons there is so little meditation on the Scriptures in the church today is because teachers have unwittingly taught their hearers to put emphasis on their own intelligence and discipline when studying the Scriptures."[21] The reality is that we will never understand the Bible the way God intended if we depend on our own intellect and discipline — only the Holy Spirit can guide us through His word and make it come alive with meaning. Allowing Holy Spirit[22] to be our guide removes the intimidation that often attends the discipline of Bible reading.

In John 5:39, Jesus declares that knowledge of the Scriptures is the path to knowing Him well. The truth is that the Bible is spiritually discerned (1 Corinthians 2:14). That means we must hear God's voice in order to understand the truth of His written Word.

A case in point is my own husband's experience. I've asked him to share it in his own words: "At age 48 and disappointed with how life was going, one evening sitting on the couch I asked to be filled with the Holy Spirit and I truly meant it. What happened next was more like what I expected when I was water baptized. Afterwards the Bible read completely different, a spiritual side of me finally came alive; everything changed. I questioned all my past, what I was taught, how was I taught, was there an agenda behind what I had been taught, what is the real truth to the matter? What was amazing is that the Holy Spirit would answer those questions for me." ~ Derf

The Pharisees in Jesus' day were full of the knowledge of what the Scriptures said. However, when Truth (as a Person) was standing right in front of them in an earthly body they relied on their own interpretations to reject Jesus. When His way of doing things greatly conflicted with their expectations and interpretations they refused to open their hearts to hear what Jesus was saying.

Contrast that reaction to Peter's rooftop experience in Joppa (Acts 10) when he fell into a trance, saw a vision and then heard God's voice. What was being challenged in this vision was one of Peter's most basic understandings of Scripture. However, Peter permitted the Holy Spirit to correct his own wrong interpretation of Scripture. Likewise, when Paul was confronted with the living Christ on his way to Damascus, he permitted his understanding of Scripture to be turned upside down to accommodate the truth.

One of the keys to my husband's spiritual growth in understanding God's Word and learning to hear God's voice was that he was willing to challenge his own interpretations of the Bible he had been reading since he was a youth. Derf had decided to allow the Holy Spirit to correct any misinterpretations, he didn't argue with Holy Spirit to keep them because they were *sacred*. Derf simply allowed Holy Spirit free access to do one of His primary jobs — speak for the purpose of accurately interpreting Scripture.

SPEAKING THROUGH AN INNER VOICE

The inner voice could come in the form of words (which we hear with our spiritual ears as opposed to our natural ears); but it could just as easily be a nudge, feeling, prompting, spontaneous thought, vision or impression from the Holy Spirit. Some people refer to this type of communication as a *knowing* in their spirit or having a *sense* of what God is saying. All of these forms, which I'm grouping together under the heading of the "inner voice," are regularly used by God to communicate with us. We learn to hear God's voice as we pay attention to the spontaneous thoughts and ideas that come to mind.

Examples of inner voice communication

"When the Lord speaks to me it is a voice talking to me inside my head. I have never heard the Lord like a loud speaker would sound or a voice like you and I talking with each other. Instead it is typically a normal sound to my ear at about the same audible level as a normal voice, except inside my head. I have had the Lord speak to me louder than normal when He wants to get my attention." ~ Bill

"I remember clearly that the first time I ever internally heard God's voice was probably my freshman year in college. I was crying out and asking Him if He really was real. I was actually surprised by the inner voice that I heard say: '*Yes I am!*' I only heard those words inside me, there was no audible voice, but those words helped settle that nagging question I had. At that time, I didn't even know God spoke in a way that people could hear — I just knew it was Him even though I had never been taught that He speaks like that." ~ Kimberly

"The second time I heard God speak to me was a time when I went out running. Things seemed all upside down; my freshman year in college wasn't turning out anything like I thought it would. I was looking down at the river feeling like life was a mess and thinking what am I going to do? George Washington University was not working out the way I wanted to; I had put all my 'eggs in one basket' so-to-speak and now I didn't know what else to do. I was in deep reflection; but I really wasn't even asking God about my life and yet I heard very clearly '*Go to Ohio State University.*' That's the last place I wanted to be. So, I knew it wasn't my voice. Since that time, I've learned that when I hear clearly something I wasn't really expecting to hear it is often God's voice speaking." ~ Kimberly

God's voice as a nudge or prompting from the Holy Spirit

"To celebrate our second wedding anniversary my husband Randy took me, my sister and my mother to Las Vegas. The morning after we arrived, Randy returned to the hotel room after breakfast saying he was not feeling well. My sister, mom and I decided to go ahead and explore Las Vegas. The next morning Randy decided to stay in bed saying he was still not feeling well, so I bought some flu medicine from the hotel gift shop. After making sure he had everything he needed, I went to breakfast with my sister and mother. After breakfast the three of us were discussing our plans for the day. Suddenly, I had an overwhelming feeling and seemingly out of nowhere I found myself exclaiming "I've got to go check on Randy!" Without further explanation I took off running, leaving my family members on the sidewalk.

When I returned to the room, I helped Randy get up and take a shower. A moment later he was having what I would learn was a seizure. I called down to the front desk and frantically asked them to send an ambulance. When the paramedics arrived, he was rushed to the hospital and diagnosed with bacterial pneumonia. The infection had spread into his blood stream and he was in septic shock. His condition was so serious the doctor said he would have died if we had waited another hour. I can't explain why I felt the urgency to go and check on him. I didn't hear a voice. I didn't feel a push. I just knew I had to get to him. I later realized it was God urging me and I was so thankful." ~ Melissa

From my discussions with other followers of Christ there seems to be at least two consistent characteristics of this form of communication: first, it is easy to dismiss and secondly, it generally makes no sense to anyone except the recipient.

"Sometimes I can't even articulate it, but I just know in my heart, 'that was God.' I try to explain it to someone and I can't. It doesn't make sense when I put it into words, but in my inner heart I feel and know, 'that was God.'" ~ Colleen

I believe what Colleen is describing is commonplace. Here's why I think that happens. That inner voice or prompting did not occur in a vacuum. In the days, weeks, maybe even months or years prior to hearing that particular inner voice you have had experiences with God's Word, worship, fellow Christ-followers, circumstances of life, prayer, etc. That inner voice doesn't occur in isolation, it layers as it were on top of all those other experiences to bring sufficient understanding. Because no one else has had precisely the same set of experiences you have had, it is understandable that they don't interpret that inner voice in the same way you do.

As a case in point, let me share an experience my husband and I had with a brother in Christ during a Zoom call. I'll call him "David" although that is not his real name. As David spoke to us about challenges he was currently facing in his ministry I had a strong impression from Holy Spirit that I needed to ask him whether there was a dedicated prayer partner[s] praying for his ministry. He assured me there was a team in place and he regularly communicated with them. Even so I sensed a need to ask him to be alert to what God may bring to his attention about the prayer team — for some reason Holy Spirit was giving me a strong impression that the prayer team was in some way connected to the ministry challenges he was presently facing. We concluded our discussion and we all prayed together before ending the call. One of the things I specifically prayed for was that God would make clear to David whatever was on His heart about that prayer team. The next day I received an email from David which I'll quote in part here: *"As I went down the hall after our [discussion], the image of James Reason's Swiss Cheese Model of accident causation appeared in my mind's eye. It's because of what you said about the prayer team. I saw the hole that is the gap in the prayer ministry. If you look at the simple graphical representation of the model that I have attached, I think you will see how self-explanatory my point is. So, I already understand the significance of what you said and am grateful."*

A graphic was attached to David's email which I had never seen before. It contained 4 slices of swiss cheese in a row with a red arrow through the middle of holes that perfectly lined up in each slice of cheese. There were various labels below each cheese slice. The graphic had the title *"James Reason's Swiss Cheese Model"* which I later learned enjoys widespread recognition across a variety of organizations. Because of David's personal familiarity with this model, Holy Spirit was able to bring it to his recollection in answer to our prayer. Even though David was confident I would be able to see the meaning of that illustration as plainly as he did, the reality is that my experience with that graphic was not the same as David's and therefore it held little meaning to me! I had to turn to the internet to be educated on the meaning of that graphic, but even then, I am certain I did not see the answer to our prayer in that graphic with the same clarity David did.

In this example of how Holy Spirit brought revelation to David after we prayed, David quickly recognized what God was saying to him. However, there are times when we don't understand that clearly. The best way to respond to an inner prompting that we do not fully understand is to refrain from trying to figure it out in a way that seems logical to us! When we are certain that prompting is from God and it contains instruction to us, we simply obey. The wisdom of man pales in comparison to God's wisdom. Paul wrote in 1 Corinthians 1:25 (HCSB) "God's foolishness is wiser than human wisdom." Unless (and until) God chooses to reveal Himself and His plan more fully there is no one who understands and it becomes an exercise in futility to pursue understanding with our finite minds.

In order to take a closer look at God's inner voice let's consider what Paul wrote to the church at Corinth:

> It is to us, however, that God has revealed these things. How? Through the Spirit. For the Spirit probes all things, even the profoundest depths of God. For who knows the inner workings of a person except the person's own spirit inside him? So too no one knows the inner workings of God except God's Spirit. Now we have not received the spirit of the world but the Spirit of God, so that we might understand the things God has so freely given us. These are the things we are talking about when we avoid the manner of speaking that human wisdom would dictate and instead use a manner of speaking

taught by the Spirit, by which we explain things of the Spirit to people who have the Spirit. Now the natural man does not receive the things from the Spirit of God — to him they are nonsense! Moreover, he is unable to grasp them, because they are evaluated through the Spirit. But the person who has the Spirit can evaluate everything, while no one is in a position to evaluate him. For who has known the mind of ADONAI? Who will counsel him? But we have the mind of the Messiah! 1 Corinthians 2:10-15 CJB

Here Paul is describing the ministry of the Holy Spirit in the life of a disciple, enabling us to comprehend the things of God. How can we know of a God we cannot see and whose thoughts are higher than human thought? The answer is: Holy Spirit. The Holy Spirit is the "Spirit of God." Just as man's human spirit knows the deep thoughts of the man, so God's Spirit, the Holy Spirit, knows the intimate things of God. During His earthly ministry Jesus spoke many things to His disciples which they did not understand or even remember. Jesus told them that after His return to His Father, He would send His Spirit. The Holy Spirit would not only bring to their remembrance things Jesus had previously spoken, He would also enable them to understand those things (John 14:26). Because of the ministry of Holy Spirit, they would be able to teach those truths to others. Jesus knew His disciples would not be able to understand everything He wanted them to know, so He told them that the Spirit would reveal things to come, things of the coming age.

"I have many more things to say to you, but you cannot bear them now. But when He, the Spirit of truth, comes, He will guide you into all the truth; for He will not speak on His own initiative, but whatever He hears, He will speak; and He will disclose to you what is to come. He will glorify Me, for He will take of Mine and will disclose it to you. All things that the Father has are

Mine; therefore I said that He takes of Mine and will disclose it to you." John 16:12-15

As we have already noted, God has an audible voice and I believe there are times when He uses that audible voice to speak to His creation. However more often I think He speaks through the indwelling Holy Spirit. When He does, I describe it like this: "His voice simply bypasses our ear gate and is received directly in our minds as clearly as if spoken by an audible voice." Another way to say it is, "the Holy Spirit who lives *in* us (1 Corinthians 6:19) speaks to the mind of Christ *in* us (1 Corinthians 2:16)."

Earlier we looked at Habakkuk 2:1 in the Jubilee Bible (JUB): "I will stand upon my watch and affirm my foot upon the fortress and will watch to see **what he will say in me** and what I shall answer to my question (bold added)." Recall that we pointed out that this particular translation accurately renders the original Hebrew text to indicate that Habakkuk was expecting God to speak *in* him not merely to or with him. We concluded this suggests that when God spoke to the prophets it was an *internal speaking* and not one that was discernible from without.

Joyce Meyer concludes, "being led by the Spirit is one of the greatest benefits for the Believer. It is a wonderful privilege and assures that every Believer can hear from God personally."[23] She warns, however, that being led by the Holy Spirit requires courage and boldness because there are times when the only proof you have about something is an inner confirmation from the Spirit and the Word of God. Most of us would much rather be able to make a direct call to God on our cell phone like it is a hotline to Heaven — ask Him our questions, hear His voice audibly answering us on the other end of the line and then have confidence we know what He has said.[24] Or, in the alternative we would like God to pull up a chair and sit beside us while we ask Him our questions and write down His answers.

I would note here that while this approach seems preferable to our natural minds we only need to read through the book of

Revelation to capture the reality that even if God chose to speak to us that directly and fully we might actually end up with more questions than answers. After all, thousands of years after the apostle John recorded the visions he was given and the words he heard spoken while on the isle of Patmos scholars are still in disagreement about what it all means!

"Volunteering at our local food pantry, I befriended a lady who not only needed food but asked me to pray with her that the Lord would provide her with a washer/dryer. The Lord impressed on my heart to pray for her. One day I noticed a washer /dryer for sale on our neighborhood website. I heard God's inner voice telling me to share my friend's request and ask for a bargain price as my husband and I would pay for the appliances. The seller said if the appliances did not sell, she would call me back. In a week's time, I received a call telling me she would be glad to **donate** the washer/dryer. But then I had no way of moving it. God again told me who to call. That Christian gentleman had a truck and helpers who not only delivered the washer/dryer to the dear lady but removed the old washer/dryer that had not worked for years. The recipient of the 'miracle' was so happy and we all praised the Lord together. God really wanted to use me to bless a fellow Christian in need." ~ Shirley

God wants us to *learn* to be led by the Holy Spirit. We need to learn how to engage in spiritual discernment. God's plan is that our growth is fueled by stepping out in faith. His grace covers our mistakes. Because that is so, He expects us to learn from our mistakes and then to have Holy Spirit inspired bold confidence so that fear does not prevent us from stepping out again. Every Christ-follower can learn to live life being led by the Holy Spirit. It is a process which unfolds over time. It is a personal investment which no one can make for you.[25]

Rick Warren tells the story of a discussion he had with his 5-year-old granddaughter Cassie. She walked into his study one day and asked what he was doing. When he told his granddaughter that he was preparing to teach his congregation how to hear God's voice, she responded "oh, I already know how to do that." When he asked her how God speaks to her, she replied matter-of-factly "in my mind."[26]

Similarly, Caleb, one of our grandsons, came downstairs and announced to his mother one morning that he regularly talked to God and God regularly talked to him. When he was about 5 years old he told her that when he wakes up in the morning he doesn't come directly downstairs. Rather, he sits on his bed for a while and talks with God. Caleb told her God didn't speak out loud to him, but he knew it was God speaking so he would answer Him back.

Children already know how to hear God speak inwardly. But for most of us, as adults, learning to be guided by the inner voice of Holy Spirit takes practice. The more we do it, the more we recognize His leading.

While preparing for this study a situation came up where my husband and I needed to pray and seek God's direction on 3 different matters. Two were requests that I do a particular thing and one was a request that he do something. Honestly, we weren't really drawn to any of the activities in the natural, but we thought we had quieted our own thoughts well enough to seek God's perfect will. As we prayed, we discerned that the answer to all 3 activities was "no" — however we did not have peace about 2 of the answers. As a result, we contacted two of our prayer partners and asked them to seek confirmation that we had correctly heard the answers to those two questions. When they prayed, what God spoke to them was the opposite of what we had heard. Having that inconsistency led us to inquire further from the Lord about those two matters. As we did, we came to understand that in both cases it was His will that we say "yes" to the request. Now here is the very intriguing aspect of this experience. On the 3rd matter, the "no" we heard did not challenge our spirits so we did not seek confirmation from our prayer partners on that matter. But the other two matters we had not heard correctly and the Holy Spirit prompted us to pursue the matter further! When we set our heart on obedience, desiring God's will above our own He has ways of ensuring that we hear the right answer. The key here is that we had to pay attention to that nudge from the Holy Spirit.

Ways We Can Suppress Holy Spirit

There are ways we can put a muzzle on Holy Spirit and make God's inner voice much harder if not impossible to hear. Let's look at the important truth that New Testament writers refer to as resisting the Spirit, grieving the Spirit and quenching the Spirit.

Resisting the Spirit

Stephen accused his fellow Jews of resisting the Spirit: "You men who are stiff-necked and uncircumcised in heart and ears are always resisting (*antipipto*) the Holy Spirit; you are doing just as your fathers did."[27] This is the only time the Greek word *antipipto* {an-tee-pip'-to} is used in the New Testament. It is a very strong word which expresses active and aggressive resistance, like defiantly trying to triumph over an adversary in battle.[28]

Grieving the Spirit

The Holy Spirit is grieved by sin. Ephesians 4:30 contains an express warning against grieving God's Spirit: "Do not grieve the Holy Spirit of God, by whom you were sealed for the day of redemption." In Ephesians 4:30 the word translated as "grieve" is *lupeo* {loo-peh'-o} which can refer to very intense physical pain in your body, for example, it is the word used for the pain experienced in childbirth.[29] It can also reference pain in the form of severe mental or emotional distress. The root word *lupe*, "denotes a *pain* or *grief* that can only be experienced between two people who deeply love each other.... [L]upe would normally be used to picture a husband or wife who has discovered his or her mate has been unfaithful. As a result of this unfaithfulness, the betrayed spouse is *shocked, devastated, hurt, wounded,* and *grieved* because of the pain that accompanies unfaithfulness."[30]

In Ephesians 4 *lupeo* refers to the pain the Holy Spirit experiences when followers of Christ choose self-governance rather than being led by the Spirit and living in faith. According to Paul, bitterness is the chief way Holy Spirit is grieved. However, he also lists rage, anger, harsh words and slander, along with all types of evil behavior, as conduct that grieves the Holy Spirit (Ephesians 4:31 NLT). When Christ-followers think, talk and act like non-believers in the world, the Holy Spirit is grieved in the same way a husband or wife would feel if they found out their spouse had an affair with someone else.[31] Worldly conduct is normal for non-believers. On the other hand, worldly behavior exhibited in the life of one who professes to follow Christ shocks and dishonors Holy Spirit. The verb tense Paul used in Ephesians 4:30 warns if you are presently grieving Holy Spirit *stop* grieving Him and then continually avoid acting in ways which grieve the Holy Spirit.[32] In other words, constant vigilance is required for Christ-followers to avoid this common pitfall.

Quenching the Spirit

Paul exhorted the Christ-followers at Thessalonica, not to "quench the Spirit (1 Thessalonians 5:19)." Here the Greek word translated as "quench" is *sbennumi* {sben'-noo-mee} which means to "extinguish" like you would smother or dowse a fire.[33] Again the verb tense Paul uses here means to keep on refusing to do this and/ or to stop doing it if it is already happening! Paul's word choice reveals that he understood perfectly well that ongoing action, continuing vigilance and enduring resistance were imperative if we want to protect our ability to hear God's voice.[34]

R. T. Kendall explains the difference between grieving and quenching God's Spirit. He suggests we *grieve* the Spirit in the context of our relationships with one another. For example, when we are unforgiving or judgmental toward another person we grieve Holy Spirit. On the other hand, *quenching* the Spirit happens "when we are prejudiced toward the way the Spirit may be manifesting Himself and by not respecting His presence." Kendall reasons that fear is the most common reason Holy Spirit's fire is put out.[35]

Priscilla Shirer tells the story of her husband who got his finger caught in a rotating door at an airport. Several weeks later he still did not have any feeling in the top of his finger. A visit to the doctor revealed that he had severed a nerve in his finger which led to a loss of feeling in that particular finger. When we decide not to obey God it is like severing a nerve and it quenches the Spirit of God in us.[36]

Paul conveys the serious responsibility we have to maintain a right relationship with God's Spirit who dwells in us as true disciples of Christ Jesus. If you have never done so before, take the time to ask, *"Holy Spirit am I doing anything to resist you, grieve you or quench your power? If so, please reveal it to me so I can change."*

We can avoid resisting, grieving or quenching the Holy Spirit by our whole-hearted submission and obedience to God's will. Paul exhorts Christ-followers to recognize two different competing powers (sovereignties that compete with each other):

> For those who live according to the flesh set their minds on the things of the flesh, but those who live according to the Spirit set their minds on the things of the Spirit. For to set the mind on the flesh is death, but to set the mind on the Spirit is life and peace. For the mind that is set on the flesh is hostile to God, for it does not submit to God's law; indeed, it cannot. Those who are in the flesh cannot please God. You, however, are not in the flesh but in the Spirit, if in fact the Spirit of God dwells in you. Anyone who does not have the Spirit of Christ does not belong to him. Romans 8:5-9 ESV

The contrast between flesh and Spirit is a contrast between two different powers or authorities that can govern your life. When Paul refers to a "mind-set" he is referring to an "avowed stance, a life-shaping attitude."[37] Our mind-set will determine how we live life day to day. It will determine which power we will submit to.

God's Spirit in a Christ-follower is His "unmediated [direct, firsthand] presence" as spiritual power enabling us to hear His voice and line up with His will.[38] The Spirit is the only one who knows the mind of Christ, He knows the Father's will and He is perfectly aligned and empowered to accomplish God's will on earth as it is in heaven. God's Spirit *always* maintains a **yes** posture to God's will. It is the work of Holy Spirit in our lives that accounts for our obedience.

The promise of the Holy Spirit is a promise of God's presence in us as effective power. But did you know we each control the degree to which the Holy Spirit is able to operate in our life and do the very things God sent Him to do? For God to be fully enabled to do all that He desires, demands that we allow Him to be fully in charge! What does it take to be controlled or governed by the Holy Spirit? Simply put it requires us to fully align our will with His, our heart must mirror God's heart and then we need to keep our hands off the control knobs! That means we don't turn down the volume knob when He is speaking, nor do we turn down the power knob when He is acting! We allow Holy Spirit the freedom to lead and we obediently follow. That will ensure that we are led by the Spirit and by our obedience God will accomplish His good and pleasing will through us.

Think of it like this: you know how you can turn a knob on a gas stove from *low* to *high*? The position of that knob regulates the amount of gas flame you have available on the stove top. The Holy Spirit inside of us responds like the gas responds to the stove knob. We control the amount of Holy Spirit that is empowered in our life and the volume at which He is able to speak. Essentially, we can be *closed* to the Holy Spirit, *partially open* to Him or *wide open* to Him.

Jesus is our model and the Bible shows us He was always *wide open* to the prompting, leading and the empowering work of the Holy Spirit. We begin with the truth that Holy Spirit indwelt Jesus during His earthly ministry.

> Then John [the Baptist] testified, "I saw the Holy Spirit descending like a dove from heaven and resting upon him...." John 1:32 NLT

> Then Jesus was led up by the Spirit into the wilderness to be tempted by the devil. Matthew 4:1

It is noteworthy that we never read that the Holy Spirit ever left Jesus during His earthly ministry. In fact, He was at work leading and guiding *all* that Jesus did and said:

> Therefore Jesus answered and was saying to them, "Truly, truly, I say to you, the Son can do nothing of Himself, unless *it is* something He sees the Father doing; for whatever the Father does, these things the Son also does in like manner...." John 5:19, italics in original

> "... For I did not speak on My own initiative, but the Father Himself who sent Me has given Me a commandment *as to* what to say and what to speak. I know that His commandment is eternal life; therefore the things I speak, I speak just as the Father has told Me." John 12:49-50, italics in original

The degree to which I allow the Holy Spirit to be who He is (to be fully Himself) in me will determine the degree to which I am like Jesus.[39] When we are *wide open* to the Holy Spirit He convicts, teaches, equips, enables and empowers our obedience. The end result is a Christ-follower who accurately RE•presents Christ.[40]

Here's the caution: we can be going along in life wide open to the Holy Spirit and then as soon as we think He is leading us to do something that even *looks* like He is going to take us out of our comfort zone, we quickly reach for the control knob and turn it down. When we do, both the volume of the Holy Spirit's voice and the power of the Holy Spirit at work in us and through us are turned down! We need to learn to trust the Holy Spirit, turn the control knob wide open and then keep our hands off the knob!

Because the primary task of the Holy Spirit is to transform us so that we become the pure, spotless Bride of Christ, His work in us can be like that of a skilled surgeon using a scalpel to systematically, meticulously and intentionally remove sin. Planning to obey God when He speaks puts us in the right position to continue hearing His voice. John 7:17 assures us that everyone who *obeys* God's will can know for certain that the voice they have heard is His. On the other hand, when we fail to cooperate with the guidance and conviction He brings, we fight against God's purposes. If we do this loud enough and long enough He can choose to simply stop speaking through that inner voice. It is just like that severed nerve in her husband's finger that Priscilla Shirer talked about.

CHAPTER 4

MORE COMMON WAYS GOD SPEAKS

IN THE LAST CHAPTER we looked at three common ways Christ-followers experience God's voice. In this Chapter we will highlight the remaining nine methods which God frequently uses to make His thoughts known to a Christ-follower.

SPEAKING THROUGH DREAMS AND VISIONS

Most of us probably think of a "dream" as mental pictures that happen when we are asleep and "visions" as images we have when we are awake. Generally speaking the Bible seems to use the terms somewhat interchangeably. What's important for our purposes is that God says He communicates this way (Hosea 12:10) and from Genesis to Revelation the Bible records examples of God revealing His will through dreams and visions. Even more important, God has graciously announced His intention to speak through dreams and visions in our day (Acts 2:17, quoting Joel 2:28).

> 'AND IT SHALL BE IN THE LAST DAYS,' God says, 'THAT I WILL POUR FORTH OF MY SPIRIT ON ALL MANKIND; AND YOUR SONS AND YOUR DAUGHTERS SHALL PROPHESY, AND YOUR YOUNG MEN SHALL SEE VISIONS, AND YOUR OLD MEN SHALL DREAM DREAMS ....' Acts 2:17

No one would argue that we are presently living in "the last days." However, for many people the application of Acts 2:17 stops there. Even though they might agree there are biblical stories where God spoke through a dream or a vision and there was no doubt it was God's voice,[1] it would never occur to them that God still speaks through dreams and visions today. Henry and Richard Blackaby rightly warn that our failure to hear God speak in a particular way does not lead to a correct conclusion that God *never* speaks *that* way. "Our experience cannot be the measure by which we understand Scripture. Scripture must [always] be the standard by which we evaluate our experience."[2]

God occasionally uses a dream to speak to me, but it is one of the least common ways I have experienced His voice. I have had the experience where in a vision I *spiritually see* God's answer in my mind's eye rather than *spiritually hear* His answer. He often speaks to my husband in visions but that too is a much less frequent way God speaks to me. However, I don't conclude based on my lack of experience that God has stopped speaking in these other ways. I think it is a mistake to do so.

Sometimes a dream is very straightforward and requires no interpretation. I've heard reports of people of other faiths, for example, who see the resurrected Christ in a dream at night and the encounter is so vivid and personal that they immediately lay down other firmly held religious beliefs and profess their faith in Jesus. In dreams of a different sort, I've spoken with two different women who received very clear dreams from the Lord about children who would one day call them "Mommy." One woman saw in her dream what appeared to be twins which ended up some years later being a brother and sister close in age that she and her husband adopted against all odds. She knew with certainty that the children she saw in the dream and the children she adopted were the very same children. The other woman had a dream of a little girl playing on a playground and that little girl called her, "Mommy." When the doctors were telling her that having a second child was not likely, she had faith otherwise. God had already used a dream to introduce her to the little girl she would later have through natural birth. In all of these cases the dreams were straightforward and easy to understand without need for further explanation.

Other dreams are not as literal, they are full of symbolic things, people, places and actions which do require interpretation. Biblical examples include the dreams Joseph interpreted for the Egyptian Pharaoh's baker and cupbearer while he was in prison (Genesis 40) and the dreams he later interpreted for the Pharaoh (Genesis 41).

Dr. Mark Virkler and his wife, Patti, have co-developed teaching for the body of Christ that addresses how to correctly hear God's voice through dreams. When teaching the course titled, *Hear God Through Your Dreams,* Dr. Virkler outlines seven principles of dream interpretation when a dream appears to be symbolic.[3] I have condensed his teaching into four general principles.

Since dreams are personal, whatever symbols God uses in your dream will typically derive from your own life experience (Genesis 37 provides us with some examples). Therefore, dream interpretation begins by asking, "What does this particular symbol mean to me?"

Dreams generally correspond to matters which are presently on your heart which suggests the meaning of the dream resides in your own heart (see for example: Acts 16:6-11).

Because of the personal nature of your dream, your heart will bear witness to its correct understanding. Your heart may seem to leap for joy when it hears the dream interpreted accurately. I believe this is a function of Holy Spirit who knows the mind of God and confirms a correct interpretation of what God has communicated.

Dreams can contain revelation from God about His will on a given matter. However, Dr. Virkler advises, and I agree, it is wise to seek confirmation from God before making major decisions based on a dream interpretation alone.

"There are times when God will speak to me through a vision — at those times what I *see* is something like a movie clip. When I was younger I had decided that I would be like the Apostle Paul; I would not get married in

order to dedicate my life totally to the Lord. However, by the second time I met Kimberly I was entertaining the thought of marriage and thinking it might have been the enemy trying to tempt me away from God's plan so I treated the thoughts as spiritual warfare. As I came to slowly understand that God had a different plan for my life than the one I had chosen, I became convinced that Kimberly was the woman I was to marry. However, she wasn't as sure as I was. God graciously gave me a vision to confirm His plan and instruct my patience in this matter. I saw two hands which were being put together and then pulled apart. Seven times in this vision I saw those hands coming together and then being pulled apart, coming together and being pulled apart. That vision sustained me through a 2-year period of friendship with Kimberly when she only saw men as a brother in Christ. She would withdraw when it seemed I got too close. She finally sought godly counsel from her parents and from God and discerned that marriage was indeed in God's plan for us. We've been married for 12 years now, but looking back I can see how that vision provided the encouragement I needed as I waited for God's plan to unfold."
~ Nathan

"Usually when I'm praying and seeking direction I hear God's voice in words. However, when I'm praying for someone else I will often see a single picture of something. What I see is a still frame, not like a movie. Then as I begin to describe or explain that picture in words to the person I am praying for I gain understanding of what the picture represents. For example, as I was praying for one woman I saw a closed rosebud. That image became an encouraging word to her that as she drew closer to God she was like that closed rosebud opening its petals. In another situation I was praying for a woman and saw a hard rock with a diamond inside it. As I began to share that picture with the woman I told her I saw God chiseling away at that rock to extract the diamond. The woman quickly confirmed the message as something God had already been speaking to her about. She was very excited to have that image from God because she had not yet completely

understood the messages about rocks she had been hearing."
~ Kimberly

I sometimes laugh that God wired me together with words, lots of them, and so words are the most common way I hear His voice. However, I do recall one specific dream in May, 2014. God had begun to speak to me about writing and publishing Bible studies and I was waiting for more instruction to know where and how to begin. What I was most familiar with was what I'll call the typical LifeWay-type of study — video teaching with a participant workbook containing 5 days of homework for each week of the study.[4] But that was *not* at all what God had in mind for me and He used a dream to make that clear to me. Here is how I recorded it in my journal entry May 10, 2014:

Right before I woke up this morning I had a dream. I went to a home-type building and parked out front along the curb. I went inside to purchase a Bible study (it was the typical Bible study, a workbook with 5 days of homework that would be complimented by a video lesson). In any event, my friend Diane was waiting on someone else and that purchase was taking a long time, so I waited for her. When it was my turn, she picked up the books for the study, calculated the cost and while she was holding out the books to me she told me the cost. I reached for my purse to pay her, but I couldn't find my purse! In the dream I thought, "Oh no! Someone had stolen my purse while I was distracted talking with others. Well maybe it's not that bad, perhaps I just left my purse in the car." Then I realized if I didn't have my purse I didn't have my car keys — I wondered if I could get into the car without my keys to see if maybe I had accidentally left my purse in the car. When I walked outside my car was gone! I remembered I *did* have my purse with me in the shop, my car keys had been clipped onto my purse and whoever took my purse stole my car! I could not even use my cell phone to call and report the car stolen, or call my husband, because my cell phone was in my purse. While others in the building were beginning to make calls for me, I was praying that my car would not get very far away, that it would be recovered quickly and that no one would be hurt in the process — that the person who stole my car and everyone else would be kept safe from injury. Then I woke up and immediately I knew I had been dreaming.

As I was pondering the meaning of the dream (realizing that a car in a dream often represents ministry) my eyes were directed to something on a ministry website I often visit. It was another person's dream along with the interpretation of that dream. Both actually helped me interpret the dream I had. I came to understand the stolen car represented a warning about stolen ministry. I had been thinking all along that if/when what I write/teach gets published it will look like the typical LifeWay-type of Bible study — a workbook with 5 lessons and a video teaching. The dream was warning me not to get stuck in that type of mindset (in other words the mindset reflected by the type of Bible study I went into the building to purchase). To do so will be a distraction from God's plan. Moreover, the ministry that He has for me will be stolen, along with my identity (represented by my purse that had my driver's license and all my credit cards & other identifying info in it). If that happens my ability to directly communicate with God will also be interrupted (represented by my stolen cell phone). Additionally, I came to understand that the type of publishing God has in mind may be something new to me (although possibly not new to others). I will need to quickly adapt my thinking and learn how to successfully and efficiently navigate the new environment.

Seven years later I can look back and see the wisdom of God's warning to me in that dream. I have written eleven studies and not a single one of them is in the format that had become so familiar to me. God has led me in a completely different direction which has unfolded into a unique style and form of Bible study. As for publishing these studies, even that was something I could not have anticipated. Publication, as it turns out, has been unfolding in two interrelated, but separate, stages. The first is to "publish" the study by teaching it, sometimes internationally, but more often in a local church. Only after publishing a study *orally* can it be released to the Christian book publisher for *written* publication. If we listen with expectation, God will tell us of His plans for us. However, when He does, we need to let those plans take shape according to His perfect will and in His perfect timing.

Almost as if on cue, while writing portions of this study God spoke to me through a dream of a different sort. I saw myself distributing the written draft of the study to about a dozen or so of my Christian sisters with an invitation to share their personal experiences of hearing God's voice. When I awoke, I not only recalled the dream, but as I pondered it I became convinced that God was showing me what He wanted me to do. After I had time to pray about it with my husband, seeking clarity and confirmation, I sent out my e-mail invitation asking each woman identified in my dream to prayerfully consider whether God was asking her to share something of her experience which could be added to the study. Then I sat and waited with excited anticipation of what God would do. Many of the testimonies in this study came from those e-mail invitations!

I know of a woman who began in her mid-80's to realize she was hearing God's voice. She was also having some dreams and understanding that God was speaking to her through them!

SPEAKING THROUGH OTHERS
(EITHER WISE COUNSEL WE SEEK OR GENERALLY)

We'll turn to the book of Proverbs for our introduction of this common method of speaking.

The way of a fool is right in his eyes, but a wise person is one who listens to counsel. Proverbs 12:15[5]

Where there is no guidance, a [group of] people falls,
but safety [lies] in a multitude of counselors. Proverbs
11:14[6]

God does not have "educational, age, or gender prerequisites
to be [his] spokesperson .... Christ can use any person he chooses
to be his messenger."[7] God has formed and shaped His body to be
dependent on each other. There are times when we may choose to
approach a trusted fellow Christ-follower to seek his or her wise
counsel. Other times God may simply sovereignly choose to send
someone to us with His message. In those times God may want
His instruction, direction, exhortation, or confirming/comforting
word to be highlighted by the supernatural way in which He chooses to sovereignly deliver it.

While teaching in another state a woman I knew asked
me if she could share something. Charlene shared
that the Holy Spirit had prompted her to bring a certain item that she had at home and give it to me because I
would know what to do with it. Later in the day when I opened
the gift it was a ceramic mug in a decorated tin. Beautiful but-
terflies adorned both the cup and the white tin can. The next
day God guided me to the *Small Straws* website I sometimes
visit so I could read that day's prophetic word. The message
was a direct counterpart to the butterfly gift I had received the
day before. Even so, I still didn't know why the gift had been
given to me or who it was for. So, I prayed and waited for God's
direction. Sometime after returning to Florida God revealed to
me who that gift and prophetic Word was for. As I met with the
intended recipient I knew that the reason God had used Charlene in such an unusual way to speak to Ann (not her real
name) was because He wanted to assure Ann of His presence
in her life. In other words, the supernatural way in which He
had chosen to deliver His message to her was actually an important part of the message itself.

"While flying to Mazatlán, Mexico for a mission trip, I
was praying about the trip when I received a vision

from the Lord. It was like a movie playing in my mind. It was clear to me that the vision was about reproduction. I thought it related to our mission trip and that it might be a word promising successful evangelism during our ministry in Mazatlán. As a result, I asked God which leader I should share this vision with. God specifically told me to tell 'Chris.' When I shared the vision with Chris he understood immediately that the message was a personal message for he and his wife who were trying to have children." ~ Nathan

"Sometimes God uses me to deliver His message of love to another person. God will point out a person to me and then instruct me to go tell that person, 'God loves him/her.' Other times I am already having a conversation with a person and I hear the instruction from God that I am to tell that person that God loves them. This actually requires a fair amount of faith because you never know how the person is going to receive that message of God's love." ~ Nathan

One of the clearest biblical examples of God using a person to deliver His word to another person is the prophet Nathan's confrontation with David in 2 Samuel 12. In this case, David was in the midst of his sin. David didn't seek godly counsel, but in His great mercy God sent His prophet Nathan anyway.

"Through years of living for Jesus and getting to know Jesus, I continue to learn how to sense direction from God. Through much prayer, seeking and crying out to Him in genuine authentic need, He always shows up. Sometimes I immediately sense His Holy Spirit's Presence and Peace. Other times it may happen later like when a friend and I are talking and she says something (unsuspecting to her) but boldly wise to me and in my heart, in that moment, I know, it is God's provision for me." ~ Colleen

"My drug addiction led me to a prison sentence. About 3 months after I was released from prison I attended a church women's retreat. The pastor who spoke encouraged us, 'When bad things happen ask God: What is it you want me to learn in this?' Her words really stood out to me as she spoke them, but I had no idea at the time how much they would guide me in the days immediately ahead. Less than a week after I heard those words, I was unexpectedly arrested and sent to the county jail. I had not done anything wrong, the State decided they had miscalculated my release date and I had not served all of my time. In the 7 days I was in jail the words of that pastor became like a mission statement for me. This was about as bad as it could get! So, I wondered, 'God what is it you want me to learn in this?' What occurred to me was that God must need me to testify about Him to the women in that jail, so that's what I did. On my last morning before I was released again I was testifying to yet another woman but this testimony was different than the others — this time there was a knowing in my heart THIS was the woman God intended to hear my testimony. God knew exactly how He wanted me to respond when I unexpectedly found myself in jail. He used that pastor to speak just 17 words which would steer me in the right direction in the midst of a pretty bad situation. Here I am several decades later and those words are as fresh and instructive to me today as they were the first time I heard them!" ~ Rhonda

My husband is my closest and dearest prayer partner. However, over the years I have also cultivated strong prayer partnerships with a number of Christian sisters. I often, when seeking confirmation of God's voice, will ask them to pray *with* me or *for* me. Sometimes I will ask them to independently seek God's will on a matter and let me know what they hear.

In 2014 one of my most faithful long-time prayer partners came to me with a very unexpected and challenging message. I was getting ready to conclude a one-year teaching assignment on the book of Revelation. It was during this time that my husband and I had dinner with her and her husband. During dinner Diane felt prompted by the Holy Spirit to share with me something that had persisted as she had prayed for me. She told me she felt the Lord had been saying over and over: 'Debbie needs to publish and then I will expand her teaching borders.' I was stunned! I trusted Diane's ability to hear God's voice, but expanding my teaching border was not something I had been praying about or had asked her counsel on. After she told me that God had asked her to pray to enlarge my borders I asked God why He gave her an assignment that I knew nothing about. Why didn't He give *me* that assignment first? His immediate answer was telling, 'Because I knew you would not pray it with the right heart.' I recognized the conviction of the Holy Spirit. Instantly I knew God was right. I was confident and comfortable right where I was (teaching as part of Women's Ministry at Worthington Christian Church). I was not seeking a larger territory! Through that experience I learned a valuable lesson. When you won't let God push you into the next level, you are arbitrarily keeping your boundaries too narrow. He will use someone else who will believe for you to push you into the next level! In this case He used my friend and prayer partner Diane to give me that push.

There is an important caution I would note about seeking counsel from others. First, it is natural to assume that if what you are hearing is from God that others, especially those who know you best, will be all for it! However, quite the opposite can be true. Sometimes those who know you best are unwittingly used by Satan as "border bullies" to prevent you from taking a bold step of faith in obedience. They mean well and think they are trying to protect you, but they may be the very ones who try to prevent your forward movement in God's plan.[8] Bruce Wilkinson points out that "some of the most convincing Bullies you'll ever meet are the people who know you and love you. Just seeing them standing in front of you with NO written all over their faces can be quite a shock."[9] Two biblical examples come to mind: Peter chastised Jesus when He said He was going to Jerusalem to suffer and die (Matthew 16:21-23); Paul's friends tried earnestly to dissuade him from going to Jerusalem after Agabus prophesied Paul's imprisonment there (Acts 21:10-14).

In 2017 God began opening doors for Derf and me to step into an international teaching ministry. It was something He had been speaking to us about since 2009. As we shared with others the baby steps forward which we began to take in that direction, a common response from friends who know us and care about us was one of genuine concern for our personal safety and well-being. If we would have relied solely on their cautiously caring response, we could easily have ended up disobeying what God was leading us to do.

One way to approach the border-bully concern would be to pray and ask God *who* you should seek counsel from. This will give you confidence that God plans to speak His truth through *that* person. Thank goodness not everyone is a border bully who opposes you. When you wait for God to show you who to ask, He may direct you to someone He knows will be an affirming and supporting "border buddy" or even someone whose counsel and wisdom is so helpful they will be a "border buster" for you.[10]

By first asking God who to seek counsel from, you can also avoid some of the following pitfalls Robert Morris identifies in his book, *Frequency Tune In. Hear God.*[11]

Sometimes a person will ask for counsel from a variety of people and receive contradictory advice. When that happens, Pastor Morris cautions "it might be good counsel but it is not godly counsel."[12] God is orderly and consistent; He never contradicts Himself.

Sometimes a person will already have in mind what they want to do and when they receive counsel it's not what they want to hear. So, they will go to another person, and another person, and so on until they finally hear what *they want* to hear. This doesn't mean that they have heard from the Lord! When you seek counsel, it means you believe you've heard from God and now you're asking a trusted Christ-follower to sincerely pray about the matter along with you and provide their input. By doing so, you are putting yourself in a position where you have no will of your own, except to know the will of God.

One closing thought here: there are times when you hear someone say something that isn't even necessarily directed to you or at you yet the Holy Spirit will give you an inner witness as if to confirm, highlight or underscore what was just said. It is as if your heart stands at attention and quickens in that moment. You may even sense the Holy Spirit in a very real and tangible way. Pay attention! This is likely God speaking to you through that person.

SPEAKING THROUGH MUSIC

In the opinion of Old Testament scholar Walter Brueggemann, a life of obedience should naturally lead to a life of *"unencumbered praise."*[13] According to Psalm 150 expressing our adoration through music is one of the ways in which we are commanded to speak to God.

> Praise the Lord! Praise God in his sanctuary; praise him in his mighty heaven! Praise him for his mighty works; praise his unequaled greatness! Praise him with a blast of the ram's horn; praise him with the lyre and harp! Praise him with the tambourine and dancing; praise him with strings and flutes! Praise him with a clash of cymbals; praise him with loud clanging cymbals. Let everything that breathes sing praises to the Lord! Praise the Lord! Psalm 150 NLT

On the other hand, God can also choose to speak to *us* through music. Because worship involving music is such an integral part of discipleship, it is quite likely that most, if not all, Christ-followers have heard God speak to them through music. You can be all alone in your car with Christian music playing or in a time of corporate worship at church. God can use the entire song or perhaps just one word or one phrase from it to speak His message straight into your heart.

There are also times when it can be completely quiet and unexpectedly the words to a song begin running through your mind.

You may begin singing those words softly or in loud worship, or perhaps you hear in your spirit your favorite Christian artist singing the words. The same words may play in our mind over and over again until it suddenly dawns on you that God is speaking to you through that song.

God's use of music can be strikingly similar to receiving an inner witness — there is a knowing in your spirit that can't be attributed to anything other than God speaking to you.

I am able to look back to a time in late 1998/early 1999 when I had purchased a new worship CD and for weeks I played it every time I was in my car. Although I did not understand it at the time, in hindsight I can see how powerfully and effectively God used the words in one of those songs to literally woo my heart into a closer relationship with Him. I didn't know exactly what was happening, but I could sense my heart was being drawn closer and closer to God. I liken it to the metaphor in Proverbs 1 where wisdom cries out in a loud, persistent voice imploring every listener to follow her. That time marks the beginning of true discipleship in my life. God used worship music to lovingly and tenderly massage my heart and prepare it to hear the words a new friend would speak to me which would turn everything in my world upside down! It was in my newly oriented right-side-up world that I moved Him into first position in my life and He truly became Lord. Music played a pivotal role in the process.

Much more recently I entered into a season of extended care for an aging family member made more difficult because of cognitive impairment issues that were presenting unexpected challenges. For days on end these words from a popular worship song played over and over in my mind, "Your goodness is running after me." As I heard the words in my spirit, I would begin to softly worship by singing them back to the Lord. One day in the midst of that worship I suddenly realized what God was nudging me to do. The repetition of that phrase was His invitation that I be still and allow His goodness to catch up to me! In worship I imagined His goodness being poured out on me till it was literally overflowing. Speaking to me through that song refrain didn't change my circumstances, but it powerfully ministered to the burden in my heart that was threatening to overwhelm me!

"My daughter-in-law gave premature birth to twins in her 26th week of pregnancy. Our little granddaughter was stabilizing, but our grandson Haskell weighed only 1 ½ pounds. He had already undergone 3 major surgeries in less than 2 weeks and as he faced a 4th surgery the doctor told us he had only a 50% chance of surviving. I got into my car for the drive home at the end of another exhausting day. I was deeply grieved at the thought of losing Haskell and I needed to hear from God. It was through a worship CD I played in my car that God spoke His promise to me. As Chris Tomlin sang the words "the roar of the lion of Judah" I heard that lion roar in my heart and I knew The Lion of Judah was getting ready to stand up and roar in the midst of my need. It was God's promise to me that He would intervene and Haskell would survive. As I give this testimony, Haskell and his twin sister, Savannah, are now 2 years old." ~ Rhonda

SPEAKING THROUGH CREATION

God's glory is manifest (made known) in His creation; therefore, it should not surprise us when He uses what He created to speak to us. It is not uncommon to talk with people who received a message from God through a sunrise, a sunset, a butterfly or some other part of nature.

"It was a beautiful, crisp fall afternoon with the sun shining brightly over a forest of crimson and gold trees. The sky was clear and crystal blue. I sat by the bedside of my mother looking out the window from the eighth-floor hospital room. I had just been told that she was dying and that I should call in the family. My heart was immediately filled with a combination of unbelief that this could be happening, searing pain, sadness, and most of all fear. I had never felt more alone in all my life. I bowed my head and closed my eyes praying and asking God to give me strength, wisdom, and release from this all-encompassing fear. As I opened my eyes I looked to the sky to see an astonishing sight! There in the cloudless, blue sky was the most glorious rainbow I had ever seen! Peace and comfort filled my soul. Gratitude filled my heart. My God was once again faithful to His promise. I knew that He would never leave me nor forsake me and though I was going to have to face this trial, He was right there beside me to see me through it!" ~ Diane

"The moonlight at night would shine in such a way that it's light on the bars of my prison cell window reflected on the glass in the shape of a cross. On those evenings I would see that reflection and would say to myself, 'When I see the cross I know I am where I'm supposed to be.' About six years after I was released from prison I was looking at a home to purchase as the first women's ministry home in *His House Ministries* — a drug recovery ministry God had called me to begin. As I entered that house I saw an Emmaus cross hanging from the chain on a ceiling fan and whispered to myself, 'When I see the cross I know I am where I'm supposed to be.' THIS was the house I was to purchase. We now operate 8 homes for women who are looking to recover from drug addiction by learning to make Jesus the Lord of their life." ~ Rhonda

One of my favorite lessons from nature comes from a weekend stay God directed Derf and I to enjoy at Black Bear cabin in the mountains of West Virginia. When we arrived at the cabin I noticed there was a mountain stream running directly behind the cabin. I walked over to it and stood on the bank trying to imagine what many of these streams would sound like. After all this was rushing water you could hear and the Bible uses the sound of "many waters" as a description of God's voice.[14] Later in the day it began to snow. Because it had rained earlier in the day the snow was not accumulating. However, it continued to snow overnight and when we awoke early the next morning there were several inches of wet snow on the deck railing, the trees and the ground. As I looked out at the beautiful site, God explained one of the most valuable lessons I've ever heard about His voice. He said, "You always want my voice to sound like that mountain stream — clear, crisp, immediate and easy to understand. However, more often than not, my voice is like that snowfall. It quietly builds up over time until the fullness of time comes and you can discern what I have been speaking to you."

All too often it is easy for the enemy to convince us God is not answering our prayer or our question because we don't hear an immediate answer. But God says that more often than not, He is taking His time to build up the answer in our heart and when the fullness of time has come (just like that snowfall) we will discern the answer.

SPEAKING THROUGH PEACE

One test of hearing God's voice is to ask whether you sense God's peace in the voice you heard.

A sermon at Calvary Chapel included a wonderful example of how God speaks through peace in our hearts to provide instruction.[15] The pastor described a decision that he and his wife were contemplating. They had prayed, felt confident in proceeding and had told a company representative they would hire them for the work. However, during the night the pastor explained that his sleep was interrupted repeatedly with a sense that they were not making the right decision. All night he heard statements like, "It's the wrong decision, you didn't wait long enough to get the right decision. This is not the right company." However, when he awoke he wasn't sure whose voice he had heard during the night – God's or Satan's. He and his wife prayed again to discern the source of those warnings. He explained, "as my wife and I prayed, I understood it was the Holy Spirit who had spoken to me. Holy Spirit said, 'Don't do it, it's the wrong timing and the wrong company.'" The pastor called the company representative and apologized that they were cancelling their contract. He explained the instant he said that to the company representative the peace of God came right over him. Because of the presence of that peace, he had confirmation that God had spoken to him and he had confidence that the change of plans was the right decision!

The author of Hebrews refers to God as "the God of peace."[16] The word "peace" is the Greek word *eirene* {i-ray'-nay} (from *eiro* meaning to join or bind together that which has been divided or disconnected). *Eirene* literally pictures the joining together of that which had been separated with the result that the formerly divided parts are one again.[17] Through the cross God opened the way for us to have fellowship with Him. When He speaks in the context of that fellowship, peace *always* attends His voice. However, when God instructs us to do something outside our comfort zone we can respond with fear or unbelief or a host of other emotions. We need to distinguish our *reaction* from God's voice with its associated peace. This can be hard to do initially, but with experience it becomes easier and easier.

There are several key Scriptures that will be helpful to us in our understanding of how God speaks through His peace. The first is Philippians 4:6-7:

> Be anxious for nothing, but in everything by prayer and supplication with thanksgiving let your requests be made known to God. And the peace of God, which surpasses all comprehension, will guard your hearts and your minds in Christ Jesus.

Once again, the Greek word translated as "peace" in Philippines 4:7 is *eirene* which in this context expresses the idea of not allowing outward circumstances or pressures to impact you. "When a person is dominated by *eirene* ("peace"), he has a *calm, inner stability that results in the ability to conduct himself peacefully, even in the midst of circumstances that would normally be very nerve-racking, traumatic or upsetting.*"[18] Biblically, *eirene* is entirely God's work because real peace comes from God and is an inward work of His grace.[19]

In Philippians 4:7 the word "guard" is a translation of the Greek word *phroureo* {froo-reh'-o} (from *phrousos*, "a sentinel, guard"). It means to guard (keep watch) like a sentry. *Phroureo* was a common military term in New Testament times. It was used to refer to posted military guards. These sentries closely safeguarded what they were assigned to protect. They typically were armed with some sort of weapon allowing them to take whatever measures were needed to protect what had been placed in their watchful safekeeping.[20] *Phroureo* is used figuratively in Philippians 4:7 (as well as in 1 Peter 1:5) picturing a posted sentry who actively and continuously guards to protect from hostile invasion. In other words, when we refuse the anxiety being offered to us by Satan and present our requests to God with a thankful heart, *then* His peace will act like an armed sentry walking his post in front of the door of our heart and the entrance to our mind. That peace will safeguard our heart and mind permitting us to look to God with confident, expectant hope that He hears and will provide in His way and His time for every request we have presented.

In John 14:27 Jesus said:

> Peace [*eirene*] I leave you; My peace [*eirene*] I give to you; not as the world gives, do I give to you. Do not let your heart be troubled, nor let it be fearful.

Paul instructed Christ-followers in Colossians 3:15 to:

> Let the peace [*eirene*] of Christ **rule** in your hearts ...., bold added

I'd like to focus on the second Scripture here which is found in Paul's letter to Christ-followers in Colossae. Let's look at the word "rule" in bold text which is a translation of the Greek word *brabeuo* {brab-yoo'-o}. When Paul admonished these disciples to let the peace of God *rule* in their hearts, the word rule means so much more than simply having the presence of peace.

Brabeuo originally referred to an umpire's responsibility to direct athletic games and decide the winner.[21] That person acted like a referee or an arbitrator who renders a verdict. Figuratively *brabeuo* pictures Christ providing assurance/confirmation to His disciple that they are properly aligned with His will.[22] In the original Greek text of Colossians 3:15, the verb tense makes plain that Paul is emphasizing that this is to be a *continuous, non-stop* privilege for every yielded Christ-follower.

Allowing God's peace to act as an umpire is to become a lifestyle for every Christ-follower. This happens when we are led by the Spirit and walk out life in faith. Of course, that includes hearing the voice of God and then obeying what we hear. "Christ gives His peace (*wholeness*) in every scene of life to the Believer who constantly desires His *whole will*."[23] In other words, peace is one of the ways God speaks and the presence of peace which exceeds our understanding should factor in to our decision as to whether the voice you are hearing is from God.[24]

Priscilla Shirer provides this quick summary of how to allow peace and conviction to guide us:[25]

- ✓ The **red** light of conviction is Holy Spirit's way of saying "STOP"
- ✓ The **green** light of ease and peace is Holy Spirit's way of saying "GO"
- ✓ The **yellow** light of doubt (dis-ease) means "WAIT"

It is important to understand that Satan cannot steal peace from Christ-followers. However, it is possible to make the choice to forfeit peace. If you were walking in peace about a matter, then find yourself anxious, worried and/or agitated about it, you have likely forfeited your peace. The most common way we surrender our peace is to fix our eyes on the circumstances around us rather than on Jesus, the one who authored and is perfecting our faith. There is a simple solution. Pray and tell God you are sorry you have come into agreement with the fear, worry and anxiety the enemy has offered. Ask God to restore your peace and He will! Then be intentional about using the spiritual magnifying glass in your hand to fix your eyes on God alone, not your circumstances! (You may recall the deer hunting testimony of the man in our Sunday School class who at the height of his frustration and anger began to recite Psalm 42 from memory. We noted that by doing so he had effectively lifted his eyes off of his circumstances and placed them on God.)

"After many years in the same church, my husband and I knew God had shown us we were to move our entire prison / recovery services ministry from that church to another church in town where the people we were serving would be more warmly integrated and welcomed by the congregation. Although we knew we were to move, this transition would be a big deal in our small town so we determined to wait on God's timing. About a year after God had made the move clear to us, we received the sign we had been waiting for. Our church called to inform us 'it was time to move the Celebrate Recovery meeting out of the chapel to another space.' We knew *they* meant to another space in *that* church building, but because God had prepared our hearts and our ears were tuned to understanding His perfect timing, what *we* heard in those words was that it was time to *move the entire ministry to the other church*. God had graciously and clearly given us the sign we had been waiting for. There was a knowing in our hearts — one that my husband and I were in complete agreement with each other about. That peace and unity we felt about this very difficult decision was our assurance God had spoken and shown us His perfect timing." ~ Rhonda

SPEAKING THROUGH MIRACLES

In its most simple terms, a miracle is a supernatural occurrence which is intended to reveal the true nature of God's intervention in that circumstance or situation. God's goal is *not* for someone to park on the occasion of the miracle itself. The miracle is intended as a sign to propel people forward into full discipleship with a testimony that will bring glory to God. The Bible is very clear that faith based on signs and miracles is but a beginning stage of faith. That type of faith alone will not endure the tests of life. Rather, saving faith must grow and mature "from initial acceptance toward full understanding, allegiance, and confession."[26]

"Several years ago, while on a mission trip, during an outdoor conference for men, I was prompted by the Lord to the fact of an approaching storm. When I looked up, I saw a huge black cloud. He instructed me to stand at the rear of the group and pray, raise my hand towards the heavens and command the storm to go back to the sea, preventing a downpour on the attendees. As I moved my hand toward the cloud, it moved away from the attendees and, when it was over the water, the rain was released." ~ Eva (not her real name)

"There was a time when I was supposed to be working the altar at a healing service, but I couldn't because I had a very painful open wound on my foot. The doctor didn't know what it was or what caused it. He gave me pain medicine and antibiotic ointment and told me to stay off it and to elevate it. He scheduled a follow up appointment in a week. It just so happened that the day before that follow-up appointment our church had a healing service. I heard the Holy Spirit tell me to take an extra pair of shoes that I would normally wear and when I got there I was to go down front and be prayed over. So, I did and as soon as the pastor finished praying over me I felt my foot get really warm. I sat down in a chair at the back of the church and took off my shoe and removed the bandage on my foot. Where there had been an open wound there was now only a red spot and the pain was completely gone. So, I put on that extra pair of shoes Holy Spirit had told me to bring and went back up to the altar to start praying for other people. The next day when I went back to the doctor to show him my foot even that red spot was gone. The doctor said 'wow' and asked what happened. I then told him that I went to a healing service at my church the night before, got prayed over and was healed. The doctor just looked at me and then my foot and said 'wow'! I guess he didn't know what else to say, so he simply said to come back if the sore returned and he left the room." ~ Phil

Good friends of ours were scheduled to leave for a week long family vacation. However, within days of leaving Darrell felt the familiar twinge of a developing kidney stone. He had experienced them before and they always required surgical removal. He decided to go for a scan to see what was happening. Quite to his disappointment, the scan showed a stone in his left kidney. Derf and I asked if we could pray for healing. Darrell and his wife, Diane, quickly agreed as they were then vacillating about the wisdom of travel under the circumstances. As we prayed there was a sense of confidence that was more than a flesh-natured belief. They left the next day and Darrell experienced no pain or problems during their week-long vacation. When he returned he had another scan and sure enough that stone in his left kidney was gone. God had supernaturally *blasted* it into small enough pieces to be naturally released from his kidney without the customary need for surgery.

Darrell and Diane began immediately to share a testimony of God's healing power. On the other hand, C. S. Lewis concluded almost 75 years ago that when a person's philosophy or theology excludes the miraculous, no number of miracles will change his mind.[27] In response to a miracle that person may explain it away or excuse it away. They may even attack the credibility of the report itself, arguing that the miracle never happened or that it was completely misrepresented.[28]

SPEAKING THROUGH REPETITION

When God uses repetition to speak to us He often echoes a particular word, thought or a verse from the Bible over and over and it seems to literally turn up everywhere. The repetition can happen in rapid-fire sequence or occur over the course of days, weeks or even months. Similar to the other ways in which God chooses to speak, hearing His repeating voice is completely unplanned by us and totally God-directed.

God can repeat the very same thing (for example: a word, a phrase, a song, a scene from nature) over and over, or He can string together similar or related ideas. Eventually the Holy Spirit will call our attention to the repetition and then it dawns on us that this is more than mere coincidence, God is getting our attention. He is communicating to us. In this case, His message is often contained in the word, phrase, idea that He has been repeating.

Pam Farrel, Christian author, provides this example, "I remember God wanting to address my short fuse. I would turn on the radio and the preacher would talk about anger. I would pick up magazines and find articles on anger. I even yelled up the stairs to my sons to quit yelling and the youngest said, 'Mom, I don't think God likes it when you yell.' *Okay God I get the message!*"[29]

I have a sister in Christ who was appointed by the Governor to be on his cabinet as the Executive Director of a newly formed state agency. Leading up to that appointment her challenge was that even though she was being nudged forward step-by-step she didn't *want* to be appointed to that position. Finally, one night she was struggling once again over this issue when her husband rolled over in bed and said to her, "Whatever it is your wrestling with God about, just say 'yes' so we can get some sleep!" His challenge to her was, "Are we going to trust God all the time with everything or just most of the time with some things?" He told her *he* was confident the Lord would make His will clear to both of them. God got her attention by His relentless persistence in the matter. Encouraged by her husband's confidence she said "yes" to the interview process, received the appointment and was in the right place at the right time for God to accomplish His will in a number of important ways. She looks back on this experience and concludes, "It was a joy — and faith-affirming — to enter that process submitted to the Spirit in unity with my husband and trusting the Lord with the outcome."

SPEAKING THROUGH SILENCE

At first blush it may seem like a paradox to say that God can speak through *silence*. I've heard this referred to as the "waiting of God." Our sense of timing and God's are often worlds apart. In the flesh we almost always have a sense of urgency when we present a request to God in prayer. For the first few minutes it might be easy to wait on His answer. However, generally speaking the longer God is silent on the matter the more impatient our flesh becomes. In our sense of urgency, we often think "someone needs to do something" and if God is not answering then we'll proceed in the direction we think best. As we proceed we will ask Him to bless it or ask Him to stop us if we should not be going in this direction. In fact, in seasons of waiting it is easy to begin to accuse God of wrongdoing. Actually, the enemy will whisper to us that God is holding out on us because of His silence. That lie of the enemy has no substance to it unless and until we begin to come into agreement with it. If we begin to agree with that lie, we will begin to think God has abandoned us and accuse God of wrongful, harmful delay.

Nothing could be further from the truth! God acts in the fullness of time. His silence is **not** a sign of His absence. "God's timing never leaves things unfinished, and it always produces the maximum effect."[30] His timing is eminently perfect and even in seasons of waiting He is at work accomplishing His perfect will. Even so, *our* timing is rarely *His* timing. Job's experience is particularly instructive for us in this regard. Job lost everything — his family, his health, his friends, his wealth and his social status in his community. However, for the first 37 chapters of the book of Job, his cries for God's help and relief were met only by God's agonizing silence (and the unwise counsel of his friends who tried to fill what seemed to them to be a void). When God, in the fullness of *His* time, answered Job His answer was instructive, restorative and perfect in every way.

I believe training our flesh to wait on God's answer is often one of the most challenging stretches of faith He asks us to make, but I also believe God is glorified greatly in our patient waiting. I remember remarking to my husband quite a few years ago, "Have you ever noticed how much God is into waiting and I'm not?" Over the years I have learned to think differently about the silence of God. When we don't hear an answer to our question, then I can trust that I don't *need* that answer yet. I may certainly *want* it — but His silence is assurance that I don't yet *need* to have it.

God's silence is one way in which He can instruct me to stay the course. God is a "just in time God." He is never late, but because He does not act prematurely He is rarely ever early either! As He teaches us to wait patiently and confidently on Him, His silence *is* His answer. When He is silent just wait, do nothing until He brings the answer and shows you what to do. If you are praying about a change, then continue to do the last thing He told you to do until He brings the answer you are seeking. Over time, with practice, waiting and hearing Him in His silence becomes easier. As we die to the needs of our flesh, our self-indulged sense of urgency gives way to God's perfect wisdom and timing on the matter at hand.

SPEAKING THROUGH CIRCUMSTANCES
(INCLUDING UNPLEASANT CIRCUMSTANCES)

Sometimes God may speak to us through circumstances or events that are pleasant and affirming.

In September, 2016 Derf and I were on the last day of our third prayer assignment in Washington D.C. for that year. As we were walking back to the metro station with our team, I noticed a metro fare card right at my feet on the sidewalk. Because no one else was around, I stopped, picked it up and tucked it in my purse. Thinking it had been depleted and tossed aside I had in mind that I would hand it to someone who might need to make their initial purchase of a card (which cost $2.00). During our ride back to our hotel, it occurred to me to check the card to see if there was a balance on it. At our metro stop the card reader showed there was a cash balance of $6.25 on that card. There was an immediate prompting in my Spirit that God was showing us we would be returning to D.C. again. As I write this testimony, it is in October, 2017 and we are on our way back to D.C. for another prayer assignment. God used the circumstances of finding that fare card to put us on notice that we would have yet another prayer assignment in the city.

One of the first Bible studies I taught was a study I had researched and written tracing the marriage paradigm through Scripture from Genesis to Revelation. One thing God showed me to do was to bring a single pink rosebud each week, then to ask the women to write their name on a slip of paper and place it in a basket. At the end of class I would ask one of the women to draw a name to see who would receive the rose that evening. I vividly recall two specific examples of how God spoke through those rosebuds. The two illustrate just how personally God can communicate. The very first night of class, the woman who received the rosebud approached me to share that very day was the anniversary of her daughter's death. She had been quite mindful of it all through class; but when her name was drawn for the rose, she knew in her heart it was God's way of drawing near to her at that particular time of need. Roses (and in fact *pink* roses) were her daughter's favorite flower! That rosebud was a love letter God presented to her personally on that evening.

The second example of God speaking through one of these rosebuds is found under the "Seeking Confirmation" section of the study. Our God is immensely personal and remarkably creative in the way He speaks!

Although God may speak to us through affirming circumstances or events, the Bible also shows us another pattern — it provides examples of how God speaks in the midst of circumstances that involve trials and suffering. Throughout the wilderness journey of the exodus narrative God often used the circumstances of lack and need in order to speak truth to Israel. There were times when they lacked water and He provided. Other times they wanted food and He brought manna. When they wanted meat to eat He provided an abundance of quail. There were circumstances when their safety was threatened and He gave them protection. Over and over the Israelites magnified their lack, accusing God of abandoning them to die in the desert. The source of that thought was Satan! What first appeared to them as proof of God's absence was always a perfect divine set up for a dramatic display of God's presence, provision, protection and faithfulness.

The fact is, Scripture teaches us that God can (and in fact may very intentionally choose to) speak to us through unpleasant circumstances. However, too many Christ-followers fail to ask God about these types of circumstances. They simply assume negative events are just a part of life here on earth and so they buckle up and hold on for dear life until the roller coaster ride is over. As a result, they miss the valuable lessons of a loving God who was waiting to teach them in the hard times.

"I was a Nurse Manager of a Pregnancy Distress Health Clinic — a prolife organization in Columbus, Ohio. Being behind in yearly evaluations of my volunteer staff, I decided to take their files home so I could finish the evaluations on time. I stuffed the files in my briefcase and hurried home. When it came time to work on the evaluations I could not find my briefcase! My immediate distress of losing those files and maybe my job, led me to intense prayer. In answer to my prayer, I thought God told me I had left my briefcase in the parking lot. However, when I reached my parking spot, there was no briefcase! I stood there pouting at God for not answering my prayer. Out of nowhere an Ohio State student ran toward me with my briefcase in his hand. He explained he was studying for an exam and saw what had transpired out of his dorm window. He had taken my briefcase inside and decided to watch for my return. I thanked him kindly and gave God all the glory! Through that experience God taught me how much He loves me and wants to protect me. It also taught me to pray BEFORE I make important decisions and to trust HIM with future plans before I make plans of my own. I often have wondered if that young man was an angel of the Lord!" ~ Shirley

Not every negative circumstance in our life is dreamed up by Satan. The Bible teaches us that there are times when God permits challenges, obstacles and trials in order to lead us to repentance, to teach us about His faithfulness or to refine us. It is important to ask God to help us understand the trials we are facing so that we can discern whether we are to engage in spiritual battle to take our stand against Satan or cooperate with God. Jack Deere notes that, "Many trials in our lives are prolonged because we fail to hear what God is saying to us in the trial."[31]

When I first began to teach women's Bible studies the first several lessons were a real struggle for me. Just about every word I would speak, I heard the enemy whisper some type of condemnation in my ear. I would hear things like, "You should not have said that." "That was a confusing statement." "These women are not understanding what you are saying." "You should have said that a different way." "The women are getting lost, you are confusing them." "The women are bored, they won't be coming back next week!" This barrage of criticism went on and on and on. By the end of the lesson I was exhausted and exasperated. After about 3 weeks of this, I cried out to God in utter desperation. I asked Him what in the world was going on? I was praying, my prayer partners were praying and still this harassment had persisted. As I prayed, God answered my prayer and I came to understand that I had two choices. I (*capital 'I'*) could teach the lesson, in which case the harassment would persist. On the other hand, I could allow the Holy Spirit to teach the lesson (guiding my words, even taking me off script if He wanted to) and the enemy's voice would go away. I had been so tightly controlling every thought and word to say it just right that I was unintentionally leaving the Holy Spirit out of the equation. God wanted to teach me the freedom of doing it *His* way. Thankfully I decided God is a much better teacher than I will ever be; He knows every thought in the heart of every woman listening and exactly what He wants to say to each one. I decided to give up the control and become a vessel through which He could speak. God kept His promise! The enemy's voice was silenced from that point forward and through a very *unpleasant* experience I learned an extremely valuable lesson.

CHAPTER 5

FOUR IMPORTANT PRINCIPLES

WHILE THERE IS no one formula to hearing God's voice, there are some principles I believe are universally applicable. In this study we'll look at the top eight principles based on my own experience. Listed in the order in which they will be considered is the principle of: 1) intimate relationship, 2) willingness of heart, 3) stillness, 4) availability, 5) expectation, 6) humble attitude, 7) spoken and written voice consistency and 8) the fullness of time.

This Chapter will undertake a discussion of the first four of these principles and Chapter 6 will conclude the list of eight with a discussion of the last four principles.

PRINCIPLE #1: RELATIONSHIP

In the context of hearing God, Dallas Willard refers to our relationship with God as a "conversational relationship."[1] By that he means we talk, God listens; God talks and we listen.

You can admire others who have a close personal relationship with God. You can dream and imagine what it would be like for you to have that kind of relationship, but it will only be your experience when *you* make the effort, when you truly seek Him and love Him with all *your* heart.

"My choices are not only important to God, but He knows they will benefit me. He loves me so much He is willing to walk through that wilderness season with me, knowing I will make it through, because I belong to HIM. He is Enough, He is all I need. He is my 'I Am'. Sometimes He helps me see it was never about getting the answers I needed, but about being satisfied 'in Him' no matter my circumstances." ~ Colleen

When God wanted to speak to Israel, Moses was the one who developed a personal relationship with God and God spoke to him face to face, as one speaks to a friend (Exodus 33:11). All of the rest of the people were satisfied with Moses listening to God's voice on their behalf and then telling them what God said (Exodus 20:18-22).

In the New Testament, the relational heart that was in Moses is seen in Mary who sat at the feet of Jesus.

> Now as they were traveling along, He entered a village; and a woman named Martha welcomed Him into her home. She had a sister called **Mary, who was seated at the Lord's feet**, listening to His word. But Martha was distracted with all her preparations; and she came up to Him and said, "Lord, do You not care that my sister has left me to do all the serving alone? Then tell her to help me." But the Lord answered and said to her, "Martha, Martha, you are worried and bothered about so many things; but only one thing is necessary, for Mary has chosen the good part, which shall not be taken away from her." Luke 10:38-42, bold added

You don't have to be the pastor or a church leader to hear God speak. The one thing you need is to be in relationship with Jesus and make it a priority to sit at His feet and listen. Jesus called those who had this type of covenantal personal relationship with Him "sheep who follow Him because they recognize/know His voice (John 10:4)." The fact that sheep know the voice of the shepherd fits the normal behavior of sheep. In ancient Israel it was common for a single sheep pen to shelter more than one flock for the night. In the morning, one shepherd at a time would stand at the gate of that pen and call his sheep. As he did, only the sheep that belonged to that shepherd would respond by leaving the pen to follow him.[2] That's because sheep learn to differentiate between the voice of their shepherd and the voice of all other shepherds.[3]

The Shepherd/sheep image is a metaphor of relationship; not just any relationship, but one of belonging and intimacy. In the animal kingdom, sheep are considered to be the most obedient and submissive animal.[4] Without a shepherd sheep are helpless; the welfare of every flock is completely dependent on the shepherd's care and concern.[5] When you observe sheep and goats in the same field in the Middle East it is easy to see that goats are more naturally curious and independent, with less interest in flocking together.[6] Whereas goats can fend for themselves, sheep depend on a shepherd for everything they need.

Let's go back a step and look more closely at what Jesus said in John 10:4 about knowing His voice.

> After he has gathered his own flock, he walks ahead of them, and they follow him because they **know** his voice. John 10:4 NLT, bold added

There are generally two Greek verbs translated as "know" in the New Testament: *eido* {i-do'} or *oida* {oy'-da} [as used by Jesus in John 10:4] and the other is *ginosko* {ghin-oce'-ko}. Although the distinction between these two verb choices is not always crystal clear, in general *ginosko* refers to a knowing that grows from experience while *eido/oida* conveys *"perception, understanding, or comprehension"*[7] and indicates a fullness of knowledge.[8] In the words of one author:

> *Eido* (*oida*) then is not so much by experience as an intuitive insight that is "drilled into your heart." In spiritual terms, *eido* is that perception, that being aware

of, that understanding, that intuitive knowledge that only the Holy Spirit of God can give. It is an absolute knowledge, a knowledge that contains no doubt.[9]

Knowing (*eido*) the voice of Jesus (John 10:4) also means knowing (*ginosko*) Jesus (John 10:14) suggesting an intimate relationship that is similar to the one Jesus had with His Father (John 10:15).[10] This similarity is made clear when Jesus told His disciples:

> I am the good shepherd, and I know (*ginosko*) My own, and My own know (*ginosko*) Me, even as the Father knows (*ginosko*) Me and I know (*ginosko*) the Father; and I lay down My life for the sheep. John 10:14-15

Jesus demonstrated the ideal way to live out this type of intimate, reciprocal relationship. He told the disciples that He received revelation from His Father and by doing so He knew what to do and say.

> For I did not speak on My own initiative, but the Father Himself who sent Me has given Me a commandment *as to* what to say and what to speak. John 12:49, italics in original
>
> For the Father loves the Son and shows Him all things that He Himself is doing; and *the Father* will show Him greater works than these, so that you will marvel. John 5:20, italics in original

The verb tense Jesus used in John 5:20 "suggests that Jesus obeyed the Father by *continuing revelation*, and [John] 10:14-15 suggests that the ideal relationship John envisions for [Christ-followers] is one in which they *continually receive divine direction* as they carry out God's will."[11] Such a relationship should naturally lead to consistent obedience on our part (John 10:27).[12]

Although God is without limit, I believe He *usually* speaks in the context of an intimate Shepherd-sheep type relationship — not a casual acquaintance. We were created to be in intimate fellowship with Him. In fact, the primary difference between a disciple of Christ and a non-believer is whether the person has a personal relationship with Jesus.[13]

"When I decided to get more serious about growing as a true disciple of Jesus, I began to take Scripture more literally. Because the Bible says that "His sheep know His voice," I decided to put into practice what the Bible said. If God spoke to people, then I wanted Him to speak to me! As I took that Bible verse more literally I began to pursue it with real fervor. I would ask God questions with the expectation that He would answer me. I received some training through the Vineyard Church I was attending, but most of what I learned came through trial and error as I began to learn that inward voice of the Lord. Over time I've learned that what God says to me is usually something my mind would not have necessarily come up with." ~ Nathan

Let's consider how Christ-followers and unbelievers generally make decisions. Let's assume, for example, each needs to decide which job to take. The unbeliever will gather his facts and try to make the best decision he can. On the other hand, the Christ-follower gathers facts and asks God what *His* will is in the matter. God knows beginning from end; He is never caught by surprise. Wouldn't you prefer to make decisions based on God's revealed perfect knowledge rather than your own limited knowledge?

PRINCIPLE #2: A WILLING HEART

The key to understanding God and His Word lies with the condition of the heart.[14] God seems to enjoy speaking to people who have a heartfelt desire to hear His voice. He speaks most clearly to people who resolve *beforehand* they are going to do whatever He tells them to do. When we are asking God for clarity and not receiving or hearing any answer from Him, the first thing to do is to check our own heart condition. Ask yourself, "what are your feelings and desires about this matter?" Whatever is in your heart will have an affect (either positively or negatively) on your ability to hear God's voice and can act as a filter when you do hear.[15]

If you were to poll people who say they are waiting for God to give them specific direction on a matter you would find many people who are listening first to *hear* and then to *decide* whether they will follow the direction God gave them. This *wait and see* approach does not honor God. "God's opinion is not just one of your options. God is not interested in debating with you about your best course of action. He already knows what that is. If you only respond to God on your terms and in your timing, then you are not prepared to hear from him."[16] The heart that is firmly set to accept the answer that best serves God's purposes is the heart best equipped to hear His voice.

In the Bible the heart willing to listen is seen clearly in 1 Samuel 3:9-11, bold added:

> And Eli said to Samuel, "Go lie down, and it shall be if He calls you, that you shall say, 'Speak, Lord, for Your servant is listening.'" So Samuel went and lay down in his place. Then the Lord came and stood and called as at the other times: "Samuel! Samuel!" And Samuel said, "Speak, for Your servant is **listening**." The Lord said to Samuel, ...

In this text the word "listening" is the Hebrew word *shama* (shaw-mah') which means to hear, especially to obey what is heard. In other words, *shama* refers to hearing with your ears and follow-up with your actions. *Shama* always implies hearing for the purpose of doing what is heard.[17] I love the clarity with which one scholar explained the meaning of *shama*: "to give one's ear to the speaker's words externally and to obey them inwardly."[18] In other words, we can safely conclude that anytime we are genuinely listening for God's voice, we have already submitted our will to His!

That means that a key to authentically hearing God's voice is to fix your heart on obeying *all* things no matter how big or how small. As you do, recognize that a "no" from God provides guidance as much as a "yes" does.[19]

In fact, author John Eldredge notes, "if you cannot hear a 'no,' you will have a hard time hearing God at all or believing that what you think you've heard is in fact from God."[20] Hearing God requires us to put everything in our life in His hands. We don't abandon our desires, but we do yield them to God.[21]

> "I have learned over time that a good way to boost communication with the Lord is to be willing to hear 'no' as His answer. In fact, don't even ask the Lord a question if you aren't willing to hear no." ~ Nathan

It is not uncommon for people (even Christ-followers) to continue to debate using the world's logic and reasoning for why it makes sense to do — or not do — something while at the same time *saying* they wanted to hear and obey God's voice. For example, I watched two close friends intellectually wrestle back and forth for a long season with their retirement decision — all the while saying, "*I want to hear God's will.*"

Blackaby notes that the "key is not to make decisions that seem the most reasonable to you but to determine which ones align with God's will. Sometimes the two are compatible, but often they are not."[22] Continuing to deliberate the pros and cons of a decision is inherently inconsistent with truly seeking God's will on the matter. The world's way is to weigh options and list pros and cons; but God's way is to simply speak His clear expressive will in whatever way He chooses! "For God's wisdom ordained that the world, using its own wisdom, would not come to know him (1 Corinthians 1:21a CJB)." You will need to stop rehearsing the pros and cons of a decision when you want to hear clearly God's will on that matter.

Here are some other examples of what holding the world's will in your heart might sound like: "If I don't do this, who will? There is no one else qualified or experienced to do it." // "I'm not sure I have the time to add one more thing to my plate right now." // "The *pastor himself* asked me to do this, how can I say 'no'?" // "I will be letting a lot of people down if I don't say, yes." // "Everyone expects me to do it, what will they 'say' if I don't."// "If I say 'yes' I'll have to give up *xyz* in order to do it because I can't do that and this new thing at the same time."// "The class is scheduled to start next week, if I don't teach it there isn't enough time for them to find someone else." // "I haven't heard from God yet but the registration deadline (or early discount) ends today, I guess I should go ahead and sign up so I don't miss the deadline (and the discount)." // "I don't know if this is God's will, but I've already said 'yes' so how can I say 'no' now?"

Do you see the inconsistency here? If my heart is full of the *world's* will on this matter there is little room left over for God to put *His* will into my heart. In order to seek God's will you need to empty your heart as fully as you can of all other desires on that matter (this includes your own will, but it also includes letting go of the desires, plans and expectations other people may have for you in this matter). If we set aside the world's way, we are better able to attune our ears to hearing God's voice.

It is important to be alert to the possibility that you may also need to lay down your desire to have the approval of others if you truly want to hear God's will. Paul warned the Galatians, "For am I now seeking the favor of men, or of God? Or am I striving to please men? If I were still trying to please men, I would not be a bond-servant of Christ (Galatians 1:10)."

If you have trouble setting aside your need/desire for the approval of someone else, ask God to help you empty your heart of all self-will, including any desire to please others. We too often underestimate the power of the Holy Spirit to help us cultivate the right heart condition. Asking Holy Spirit to help us get our heart right before God is a prayer He will ALWAYS answer! That's His job! In fact, this is the very essence of the promise in Ezekiel 36:

> Moreover, **I will** give you a new heart and put a new spirit within you; and **I will** remove the heart of stone from your flesh and give you a heart of flesh. **I will** put My Spirit within you and cause you to walk in My stat-

utes, and you will be careful to observe My ordinances.
Ezekiel 36:26-27, bold added

This is a new covenant promise to deposit the Holy Spirit
in us who will then ensure that our will is aligned with God's
will. In fact, it is a promise that God will give us *His will* to do
His work:

> For God is working in you, *giving you* the **desire** [*thelo*]
> and the power to do what pleases him. Philippians 2:13 NLT,
> italics and bold added

Paul is writing to Christ-followers to encourage them to
grow and mature and become more like Christ. As noted, the
word "desire" in bold text is the Greek word *thelo* {thel'-o}. It
implies "active volition [desire] and purpose."[23] Paul is referring
to God's deliberate, purposeful intent to fulfill His plans.[24] He
is saying it is *God* who takes the initiative for our motivation
to do those things He has planned for us.[25] Said another way, it
is "God's power [that] makes His church *willing* to live godly
lives."[26] When we permit the Holy Spirit to impart to us the
desire and the *power* to do God's will, "then that desire and
power becomes [ours] by His gift, and [we] do His will 'from
[our] heart.'"[27] While this may sound radical, it is the very thing
promised in Ezekiel 36. Sadly, however, because *God* provides
the *desire* and *willingness* to permit His work in our lives, unless
we align with Holy Spirit we will never desire what God desires
for us. As a matter of fact, we will be oblivious to what we lack!

PRINCIPLE #3: STILLNESS

"God often speaks loudest when we are quietest."[28] Have you
ever been on your cell phone when you pass by some very loud
noise in the background? What happens? It becomes virtually
impossible to hear what the other party said until the background
noise ceases. Then when it is quiet again you have to ask the other
person to repeat what they just said. The challenge for us is that

when it comes to God talking He expects us to be still enough to hear the first time.

God can thunder! He can shout if He wants to, but I believe He most often speaks in a still small voice, the gentle whisper heard by Elijah (1 Kings 19:12). If we do not cultivate the practice of quiet surrender we will likely miss what He has to say to us. God's peace is always present in our stillness. If you have agitation, worry and anxiety while you are "waiting" on God's answer, you are not being spiritually still.

> "There have been times when I felt God was far away from me, when I didn't hear from Him, and I begged and cried, 'Lord, please, show up, please come to me now.' It would be so painful yet in that 'wilderness moment', if I allowed myself to stay there in the pain, vulnerable and broken, I would soon know, He was there with me. He encouraged me to practice Psalm 46:10, 'Be still, and know that I Am God.' You see, when I tried to make hearing from Him about me, it never worked. I had to be totally surrendered to Him and I had to 'show up', in my surrendered state of vulnerability and courage to say, 'Here I am Lord, I need You so much, I praise You today and I will continue to practice fixing my thoughts on You.'" ~ Colleen

Note that it is very hard in the natural for "flesh" to be still. It takes practice, but God (who knows how we are formed) is very patient with us — we can even ask Him to help us cultivate the practice of stillness and He will! The enemy fights hard against our stillness; he understands that it is dangerous for him when we learn to be still before the Lord. Some of the most common distractions the enemy has used with me to interrupt (and prevent me) from cultivating stillness are: food (snacking or stress eating, i.e. eating when I'm not really hungry); shopping (which consumes lots of time and energy as well as flooding our senses with worldly sights, sounds, images, etc.) and a feeling of physical weariness (desiring sleep over time spent with God). TV or social media can also be a powerful distraction for some people. If we aren't on guard for

Satan's trap, we will rush to fill the void while we are waiting — this is NOT waiting; it is fleshly activity disguised as waiting.

I was created in God's image with the ability to hear His voice; but the more I choose to "feed my flesh" with things of the world the harder and harder it becomes to hear God's gentle whisper. God is the one who creates the hunger in us so that we come to Him! Only He can satisfy that longing He has placed in us.

Another Kingdom principle I have learned from experience about stillness is that the louder my own heart's voice is on a given matter, the more I will need to still my heart before I can expect to hear from God.

Let me explain with an example: There was a time when I was asked by a ministry partner to take on the task of grant funding for them. Derf and I have experience in this area and neither of us relished the idea of saying "yes" — in fact the cry of my heart was not just "no" — it was literally shouting "NO WAY. This is very hard work and I don't have time for it!" Unless I was able to still my own heart's loud voice on this matter, I would be unable to hear God's voice about it.

Think of it this way: Have you ever been talking/perhaps protesting so loudly or so persistently that you didn't hear what someone else said? In fact, maybe you didn't even know they were speaking! It is the same way with God. So, when you have your own strong desire about something, make sure that the first thing you do is get your heart still (ask Holy Spirit to help you accomplish this if you need to). Then you can listen for God's direction and trust that when you hear Him, His voice has not been filtered out by your own heart's desire.

Priscilla Shirer tells of a conversation she had with her father when she was debating between several college choices. She confesses that she really had not prayed about the matter to seek God's will because her own will was to go to the same college her best friend was going to. However, when her father prompted her to pray about it she

dutifully did — although she admits she really did not expect
(or even necessarily desire) to hear God's choice in the matter.
Right after she prayed with her father, the phone rang in her
bedroom. It was her best friend who wanted to share with her
that she had prayed and asked God to provide a full scholarship to whatever university He wanted her to attend. She had
been all set to attend a small private women's college, but she
had just changed her choice after getting a letter that day in
the mail from a different university offering a full scholarship.
You guessed it, the university she was now planning to attend
was one of the two choices Priscilla had been wavering back
and forth on. Priscilla said she ran back to her father's study
shouting, "He speaks, God speaks!"[29]

PRINCIPLE #4: AVAILABILITY

This is not simply a regularly scheduled quiet time — it is
much more than that. Deere warns, "It is possible to have a quiet
time every morning and never be available to God."[30] This is especially true if having quiet time is a matter of doing it at a certain
time to check it off the *to do* list on any given day without giving
it another thought after it has moved to the *done* list. "People who
are truly available to God see God as owning their day. He is free
to reorder it at any time He chooses."[31]

We don't get to choose "*how*" God speaks to us and we don't
get to pick "*when*" He chooses to speak. I have personally found
that the most common time God speaks to me is in the early
morning hours (most usually between 1 a.m. and 3 a.m. although
not exclusively). I once sought to understand "why" this was so
and what God impressed on my heart is that when I awake from
a sleep and come before Him in the early morning hours as He
awakens me, my mind has not yet been inundated with the sights
and sounds of the world for that day. It is fresh and perhaps in the
very best condition to hear the pure, holy (set apart) Word of the
Lord. Once I begin my day and take in sights and sounds of the
world, I may still be able to hear Him but it is easy for His voice

to be "filtered" by the world's voice.[32] Note: I have a practice of reading from the Bible right before I go to sleep. I think it is quite possible there is a direct correlation between going to sleep immediately after reading God's Word (no worldly input before sleeping) and then hearing His voice in the early morning hours.

I also find working in this principle the truth of priority — God wants to be *Lord of my life*, not merely a part of it. As a result, He has the right to ask me to choose *Him* over more sleep. One thing I have found — I have **never** lacked sufficient energy to meet my day's commitments because I arose to spend a few hours in the middle of the night with Him! Our flesh will battle this greatly — it becomes a matter of spiritual discipline to crawl out of a cozy bed and come to that meeting place with Him when He calls. He is better than any alarm clock! Nevertheless, if we keep hitting "snooze" He will simply stop calling.

CHAPTER 6

FOUR MORE IMPORTANT PRINCIPLES

S O FAR, we have looked at the principle of intimate relationship, willingness of heart, stillness and availability. In this Chapter we will conclude this section of the study with a focus on expectation, humble attitude, consistency between God's spoken and written word and the fullness of time.

PRINCIPLE #5: EXPECTANCY

We can know in theory that God talks, after all that is what the Bible says. Do you seriously anticipate that God is going to talk to *you*?

"The Bible says those who seek Him will be rewarded. When we knock, when we ask, God's word says He will meet you and speak to you. When I ask God questions, I most often hear the answer in an inner voice. I've never heard an audible voice, but the inner voice comes with great clarity." ~ Nathan

Listening, paying attention to sound received in the ear is an important part of God's created order. Those who study animal behavior, whether domesticated dogs, cats, horses or elk in the wild have observed that animals use their ears to indicate that they are listening. For example, when a horse points his ears forward he is alert; the horse is paying attention to what is in front of him.[1] When a cat twitches its ears it is often an indication that they are hearing sounds their human owner has probably missed.[2]

What God has done in the amazing animal kingdom He created, He has apparently also done for we who have been created in His image. A study by a German University has concluded that all people's ears make tiny movements in order to direct them towards those sounds that we want to focus our attention on.[3] While the study credits evolution, the truth of the matter is that it is God's intelligent design that has ordained this movement to be so.

The Hebrew language has more than one word for hearing or listening. *Shama* seems to be the primary verb, but another important word is *qashab* {kaw-shab'} which according to a leading Lexicon means to prick up the ears.[4] *Qashab* is used in the Psalms when the Psalmist cries out to God asking Him to incline His ear towards the psalmist's prayers.[5] Its use in Isaiah 34:1 is the reverse. There God instructs *us* to prick up our ears and incline them towards Him so we can hear what He has to say. *The Complete WordStudy Dictionary of the Old Testament* points out that the basic difference between *qashab* and other Hebrew words for hearing is that *qashab* indicates "paying close attention to something."[6] In the Bible it is often translated as "hearken" a largely outdated word which means "to give respectful attention to."[7]

It pleases God when we approach Him with our ears pricked up, leaned forward and twitching in confident expectation. While journaling one morning I heard the Lord say, "I will be drawn by your expectancy, I am drawn by a heart that desires to listen." The one who waits with expectation on God is one who seeks Him and the one who seeks Him will find Him!

Years ago, I learned one of the most valuable lessons I've ever learned about prayer. The lesson came from the *Experiencing God* study by Henry Blackaby. His wise instruction was that when we pray, we should connect what happens next to what we have prayed; in this way we won't miss the answer God brings. The principle of expectancy is similar. When we ask God to speak to us, we should anticipate His voice and connect what happens next to our expectation. As we do, it is more likely that we will recognize that it is God speaking and we will learn to hear His voice with greater clarity.

PRINCIPLE #6: HUMILITY

God holds us accountable for how we steward His voice. The Bible is clear that God is not pleased with pride which ultimately leads us to be self-dependent rather than God-dependent.

James tells us: "*GOD IS OPPOSED TO THE PROUD* (James 4:6a, caps in original)." The author of Proverbs warns: "Pride goes before destruction, And a haughty spirit before stumbling (Proverbs 16:18)." However, the Bible also contains an incredible promise that God "*GIVES GRACE TO THE HUMBLE* (James 4:6b, caps in original)."

Why is this issue so important to hearing God's voice and hearing accurately? Because very simply: pride blinds us to the truth and blocks or distorts our ability to hear. A filter of pride will always affect the clarity and accuracy of how we hear God's voice. The natural outcome of pride is independence from God, whereas the supernatural outcome of humility is utter dependence on Him.

The following definition of humility (slightly paraphrased in my own words) is one of the best I've seen:[8]

> Humility is a profound distrust in our humanity. It distrusts our own ability, but overwhelmingly trusts in God's ability. Humility realizes our own strength, skill, intelligence, or even our luck, isn't enough to secure success. Our successes come through God's grace, mercy and power and that should humble us.
>
> Humility depends on the power of the Holy Spirit to intervene in our circumstances, not our own ability to maneuver.
>
> Humility depends on the Spirit's ability to speak, not our capacity to hear.
>
> Humility depends on the Spirit's proficiency to lead, not our skill to follow.

Everything God does He does for His Name's sake. His goal is to be glorified, because only when He is glorified can the world see Him and come to know Him as He really is. When, as His disciples, we try to do things independently of Him we get the honor. Only when we do His will, His way, in His perfect timing do we glorify Him. This is such an important truth.

In his sermon series, *Frequency*, Robert Morris cautions that God will equip us to defeat the enemy when we walk in humility, but He can play on the opposite team and oppose us if we are walking in pride (independence from Him). We already looked at the truth of James 4:6a, God is opposed to the proud. The Greek word which is translated as "opposed" is *antitassomai* {an-tee-tas'-som-ahee} meaning "squared off (opposite to); opposed to *in principle* and *in practice*."[9]

In a military sense *antitasso* refers to ordering one's self against someone else. In the context of James 4:6 it conveys the idea of preventing the plans of the proud from succeeding. In the original Greek text James uses a verb tense which indicates that this is God's continual attitude against the proud and self-sufficient!

In his book, *Humility*, C. Peter Wagner tells the story of two men used mightily by God in the late 1940s and 1950s: Billy Graham and William Branham. Wagner notes that for twenty years:[10]

> Branham's meetings were much larger than Graham's. Branham would deliver prophecies. Seemingly at will, he would, with pinpoint accuracy, call out people's names, family members, Social Security numbers and other private information. After his meetings there would be huge piles of crutches and rows of empty wheelchairs left by people who had been healed — something unseen at Billy Graham's meetings. Message for message, many more people found the road to heaven through Branham than through Graham.

Even so, to this day the name of Billy Graham is synonymous with evangelism while virtually no one remembers William

Branham. Wagner researched why this was so. He concluded that while Branham and Graham both began their ministries hearing and speaking the word of God with humility, Branham began to steer off course and become increasingly prideful — "a sad departure from the simple humility in which Branham's ministry had begun."[11] In 1965 Branham died from injuries he sustained in a car accident.[12]

There are a number of things we can do as Christ-followers to protect our heart from pride. For example:

- ✓ Being continually filled with and led by the Holy Spirit is one of the best ways to attain humility[13]
- ✓ Develop the practice of thanksgiving to God — this will keep our eyes focused on Him
- ✓ Prayer (ask God to shield you from pride & keep you humble)
- ✓ Bible study
- ✓ Magnify the Lord with praise
- ✓ Be intentional about seeking God's will in *all* things
- ✓ Select an accountability partner who will pray with you and for you & can speak the truth in love to you

PRINCIPLE #7: SPOKEN AND WRITTEN VOICE CONSISTENCY

John 16:13 states plainly that the Holy Spirit "will not speak on His own initiative; but whatever He hears, He will speak; and He will disclose to you what is to come." In the same way that Jesus only spoke what He heard His Father say, the Holy Spirit will only ever speak what He hears God say.

God's voice will always line up with the Bible. That does not mean that the Holy Spirit will always speak to you with a Chapter and Verse from the Bible, but it does mean there are biblical principles which will support what you believe you have heard from God. It is unlikely there will be a specific verse in the Bible God uses to tell you who to marry. On the other hand, there are principles which will line up and assist you in discerning God's voice on the matter. As one example, the Bible states unmistakably that a Christ-follower is not to be unequally yoked (2 Corinthians 6:14).

In July, 2017 when facing a family crisis, I realized life was about to change significantly. I asked God to speak to me about who I needed to be in the midst of that particular situation. In response, I heard two things:

1) From reading the Bible, I understood He wanted me to approach Him as "El Shaddai" in the midst of my troubling circumstances. Not only is He all-powerful, He is also all-sufficient. He has the sufficiency to meet every need I have! (Note: this is one of those times I asked Him where He wanted me to read in the Psalms and He clearly said Psalm 91).

2) Two days later He woke me up early in the morning with one word: "lockstep." When I misinterpreted what He was saying (thinking it meant something like hand-in-hand or arm-in-arm) the Holy Spirit nudged me to look up the definition of the word. Lockstep is a way of marching single file with each person as close as possible to the one in front of them. It requires close adherence to and imitation of another's actions such that it minimizes individuality.

When God gave me the word "lockstep" He was saying to me — let Me take the lead; then you follow closely behind Me — closely adhere to Me, mimic Me, *only* do what I do. Lockstep is not a word you find in the Bible; but the principle it conveys is biblical![14]

PRINCIPLE #8: GOD'S TIMING

God has specific plans for each of us as He works through us to advance His Kingdom. We don't always understand His timing, but we can be sure that coming into agreement with that divine timing is always for our best. When our hearts are set on God's timing He has a straightforward pathway to give us specific direction.

For example, in order to defeat Jericho God laid out a very explicit plan to Joshua which included marching silently around the city for 6 consecutive days, then on the 7th day when they did exactly what God said to do the city walls collapsed. The Bible is full of similar examples of God's perfect timing.

I recall one year just before Derf and I left for an extended vacation I had stopped by a pet store to get an idea about what a cock-a-poo puppy cost. I had no idea at the time that store practice was to retrieve the puppy from its crate, then hand it to the customer to hold while answering their question. I can tell you their policy works to sell puppies! They handed me that little 3-month-old tri-colored cock-a-poo and it was love at first sight! The problem was our travel schedule did not make it convenient to get a puppy at that time and the pet store would not "hold" him for us. I worked as hard as I could to figure out a way to get the puppy AND do the travel, but to no avail. Derf was wisely advising me to bypass this particular puppy and wait till we returned to get another one. The problem was, my heart was already set on *that* puppy! One evening when all my "plans" failed, I heard God say in my Spirit, "submit to your husband on this." I knew God meant I was to let go of the thought of getting that puppy. Although very disappointed, I came into agreement with God's plan and dropped the matter. It was more than 3 weeks later when we returned home and Derf said I could go back to the pet store to inquire about that dog. In my heart I had resigned myself to the fact that someone else would have bought him and I would need to look for another dog. But God! There in the first crate was that same puppy (albeit 3+ weeks older) AND there was a big orange sign on the crate that he was 40% off. Fearing he had some type of terminal illness and they just wanted to give him a good home so he could die peacefully with a family, I asked why he was discounted. The answer shocked me. They pulled his paperwork and said, "no one has asked to take this dog out of the crate in over 3 weeks! When that happens, we discount them so as to encourage their sale!" I realized God had set that little puppy aside just for us! The last person to take him out of his crate was me! I submitted to God's plan and although I didn't know it, in His perfect time His desire was to BLESS us! The puppy came home with us that night. We named him Charlie and he did indeed bless us for the next 15 years! God's timing is absolutely perfect in every way!

Another element concerning timing is the biblical principle that "time comes." And it is important to understand that God is not time bound as we are. Therefore, He can (and most likely will) speak a word of instruction or promise without indicating "when" it is to occur. Because it is not time bound, it sounds to us like an imminent command/promise — but it could be days, weeks, months, even years before its fulfillment.

This is important to understand because if we don't know that God's concept of time and ours are often quite different, it will be easy for the enemy to convince us we did not hear God speak when we actually did! Let's consider two biblical examples:

> Pharaoh said to Joseph, "See, I have set you over all the land of Egypt." Then Pharaoh took off his signet ring from his hand and put it on Joseph's hand, and clothed him in garments of fine linen and put the gold necklace around his neck. He had him ride in his second chariot; and they proclaimed before him, "Bow the knee!" And he set him over all the land of Egypt. Moreover, Pharaoh said to Joseph, "Though I am Pharaoh, yet without your permission no one shall raise his hand or foot in all the land of Egypt." Genesis 41:41-44

Joseph was probably 17 when God spoke to him in a dream showing him he would be a great ruler and his brothers would bow down to him (Genesis 37:2,[15] 5-7). He was 30 years old when he interpreted Pharaoh's dream and was made second in command to Pharaoh (Genesis 41:46). In other words, God had planned a gap of about 13 years between the dream and its fulfillment.

> David was thirty years old when he became king, and he reigned forty years. At Hebron he reigned over Judah

seven years and six months, and in Jerusalem he reigned thirty-three years over all Israel and Judah. 2 Samuel 5:4-5

When Samuel anointed David (1 Samuel 16:13) scholars believe David was about 15 years old. Samuel tells us he did not take the throne until he was 30. That means David spent at least 15 years in preparation for the throne of Israel.

Both Joseph's and David's years of preparation need to be put into perspective by considering the assignment God gave them. Generally speaking God uses a preparation time that is commensurate with the task. In other words, God's pattern is generally the greater the task the longer the period of preparation. However, the two biblical examples we have just considered did not include a complete timeline when God spoke. Neither David nor Joseph knew how long it was going to be before what God had said to them would actually take place.

I have watched God follow this very same pattern in my own life. For example, in February, 2010 we installed a new hardwood floor in a portion of our Ohio home. The day I finished putting the furniture and last of the room accessories in place I stood back to take a look. As I did, I heard the surprising instruction: "sell the house." My immediate response to what I heard was to think to myself, "sell the house? We just got the floors finished!" I called one of my prayer partners and together we agreed that this was likely not an instruction to put the house on the market right then. She and I agreed to pray about it; likewise, Derf and I began to pray about it. As the years went by I didn't hear another word about selling the house or moving until about March, 2014. I was finishing a year-long teaching assignment and was asking God what I would be doing next. I received clear direction to use my time to downsize greatly and He made it clear that "greatly" would be the key. That's all He said. In obedience, I used my time after I finished that current Bible study to begin to downsize our personal belongings; but there was still no instruction to sell the house. That didn't come until April, 2015 when God shocked us by informing us we were to move to

Pensacola, Florida! The move was made just 7 months later. Although I heard what sounded to me like a present instruction to sell our house in 2010, it wasn't until August, 2015 that God set the date for us to put our house on the market. It is important to understand this principle of timing that comes to fullness on the Kingdom calendar when God speaks to you.

CHAPTER 7

GOD'S VOICE

IN HIS BOOK, *The Pleasure of His Company*, Dutch Sheets counsels: "We must learn to commune with the Lord as a real person and on a personal level. Hearing and discerning God's voice is not a gift, but rather a learned art .... The obvious insinuation [of Scripture][1] is that our actions, not His, will determine whether or not we hear from Him. Again, sensitivity is learned and developed. Like the frequencies on a radio, our minds and hearts must tune in."[2]

New languages are not learned instantly. Language proficiency develops over time through intentional continual use. The same is true about learning the language of the Holy Spirit. It is going to take time, "but the journey begins by jumping into the deep end and starting to swim."[3] The Christ-followers who become skilled at hearing God's voice have developed their skills over a long season of listening and obeying. Jack Deere wisely advises, "If we keep our hearts open to God's correction, develop the habit of frequently asking him his opinion on matters, and then listen for his answers, over time we will become skilled at hearing his voice. Be patient. Give yourself time."[4]

We have a very real enemy who hates everything of God. He is persistently active in the earth realm today convincing God's people that they have been abandoned by God, that God does not see, He does not care and He does not speak. Satan cannot ever silence the voice of God unless we *choose* to walk in that silence. On the other hand, he will work endlessly in various ways attempting to prevent us from recognizing the true source of his voice. He seeks to wear out the saints (Daniel 7:25 AMP).

God's voice and Satan's voice are distinctly different. Learning to recognize the voice of the enemy and his lies helps us grow in our confidence that we are hearing God's voice. To that end there are some general clues which can help listeners discern between those two rival voices — the voice that leads and the voice that misleads.[5]

I realize others encourage learning to distinguish between *three* voices — our own, Satan's and God's. I believe that makes the matter overly complicated. There is strong biblical justification for simplifying our discernment to just two influencers. The thoughts we have will either be influenced by Satan who works through our flesh or God who works through His Spirit.

Let me explain: No one really knows what life was like before the fall. We do know with certainty that in the garden God made it very clear to Adam that there was one tree he was not to eat from — it was called "the tree of the knowledge of good and evil (Genesis 2:17)." Notice it is not called "the tree of good and evil" — God refers to this tree as "the tree of the *knowledge* of good and evil." The Hebrew word translated as "knowledge" is *da`ath* {dah'-ath} which is "a general term for knowledge, particularly that which is of a personal, experimental nature."[6] The root word *yada`* commonly expresses personal knowledge gained through experience by our senses.[7]

I believe Pastor Robert Morris is correct when he teaches that God never designed us to live life having to choose between good and evil. He created us to live an abundant life in perfect fellowship with Him, to hear and follow the sound of His voice.[8] In other words, we were created to live by the voice of God — the Words that come from His mouth (Matthew 4:4). The sin of Adam and Eve changed reality. Because of sin, we do indeed have experiential knowledge of good and evil and every decision we make involves that choice. There is no third choice — nothing in between; there are only two kingdoms.[9] The kingdom of darkness and the Kingdom of Light compete with each other for our worship. *Every* choice we make ascribes worth (the essence of worship) to that which we choose.

Our choices are manifested in our behavior. Behavior originates with thought. Researchers at Queen's University in Canada report that they have discovered how to measure the onset of new thoughts in a person's brain. Their research concludes that the average person has 6,000 separate thoughts per day.[10] That means that during our waking hours we will have about 375 new thoughts every 60 minutes.[11]

Every one of those thoughts will be influenced by either good or evil — Satan or God. God's Word tells us that we have the power to think about what we are thinking about; we have the power to take our thoughts captive and make them obedient to Christ (2 Corinthians 10:5). Because our thoughts precede our behavior, it is our thoughts that will determine whether we are being led by the Spirit or by our flesh nature (Romans 8:5-9).

There are some consistent clues that can help us distinguish between God's leading voice and Satan's misleading voice.[12]

THE FATHER, SON AND HOLY SPIRIT WILL ALWAYS ... TELL THE TRUTH

Jesus not only tells the truth, according to John 14:6 He embodies truth! The Greek word *aletheia* {al-ay'-thi-a} translated as "truth" in John 14:6 refers to what is factually true.[13] When Jesus says He is truth one of the things He means is that all He says is true to fact by definition. "The Dead Sea Scrolls contrast the spirit of truth with the spirt of error (cf. 1 Jn 4:6)."[14] Paul testifies to Titus that, "God ... never lies (Titus 1:2 ESV)" and the author of Hebrews points out that, "it is impossible for God to lie (Hebrews 6:18)."

THE FATHER, SON AND HOLY SPIRIT WILL ALWAYS ... BE CONSISTENT

God "is the same yesterday, today, and forever (Hebrews 13:8)." His voice will be reliably consistent. He never contradicts Himself. His inner voice / promptings will *always* lineup with His character and His Word. Moreover, His voice on a given matter can persist over a period of time in the same direction.

When we are led by the Spirit our brain is hardwired to pick up on clues from all around us, even in unexpected times and places, which enable us to understand that God is speaking and to comprehend what He is saying. We cannot possibly treat all the information that regularly surrounds us in our waking hours on equal footing. God provided a solution for that! Located at the base of our brain is a reticular activator which God specifically designed so that we can quickly distinguish between relevant and irrelevant pieces of information. Our reticular activating system (RAS) acts like an information gatekeeper telling us what is important enough to pay attention to.[15]

Our RAS pays attention to what our brain is already focusing on and then creates a filter which listens for more of that same type of information. This filter enables our brain to be sensitive to certain information and ignore other data. As a practical matter, here is how the RAS can work when God is speaking to us. Let's say that I recently read a Scripture that Holy Spirit highlighted to me, but I'm not sure why. As a result, I pray and ask God to bring revelation and understanding; but at that particular time, I don't hear anything from God. A week later I'm at a social event where people are spaced throughout the room carrying on different conversations between themselves. Across the room I hear a word that sounds familiar — it is one of the key words that was in the Scripture I have been waiting for God to explain. I move across the room and join that conversation. There I receive additional insight into that portion of Scripture. The reason I picked up on that word across the room is because my RAS acts like a metal detector in my brain. It is constantly scanning all the information input I receive at any given time listening for something that sounds familiar — something I have already been thinking about. When something familiar is detected I am alerted to pay attention to that information. In this way the Holy Spirit is able to lead me step by step into the revelation I'm seeking.

That conversation I joined may be the end of the matter, but it could be that God has more to say to me about that Scripture. The next day I turn on the radio as I'm working in my kitchen and my ears perk up when I hear someone read that same Scripture. I may momentarily stop what I'm doing and listen as the radio personality discusses some aspect of that Scripture God has been teaching them. Again, my RAS alerted me to the fact that this is helpful information — it conforms to something that I'm already thinking about and so I sharpen my concentration and listen intently to what is being said.

That afternoon I may be drawn to my bookshelf where my attention focuses on a particular book. When I pull it off the shelf and open it up the Holy Spirit may guide me to a specific page and then to something specific on that page — to my delight it is more information about the Scripture that I've been meditating on.

None of this is coincidence or happenstance, it is God's intentional way of speaking over a period of time in the same direction — adding insight to insight, revelation upon revelation. He often uses a variety of methods of speaking as He captures our attention and reveals piece by piece what He wants us to know.

My point is that God has equipped us to be amazing receptors of what He wants to speak to us. He has purposefully designed into our brain a way in which He is able to continually focus our attention on the consistency of what He is saying no matter what method He uses to speak to us![16]

THE FATHER, SON AND HOLY SPIRIT WILL ALWAYS ... BE POSITIVE

God is like a good Father; the majority of what God wants to say to you is encouragement. "Satan wants to drive us compulsively; God wants to draw us compassionately."[17]

"In the early years of our marriage my husband and I moved several times because of his job. During one season of our life we were members of a church that decided to start a pre-school program. The chairman of the Board asked me to consider taking the job. My husband and I prayed about it and it seemed like it might be something I was supposed to do. However, when I arrived for the interview with the Board, I learned that another woman in our church was also applying for the job. I knew God was telling me that the job was not my assignment and that I was to leave immediately. I didn't know quite how to excuse myself so I sat through the interview praying I would not be offered the job. But I was and I accepted it. There were blessings during that year, but overall it was a miserable year with a whole lot of problems. One night I was lying in bed crying softly so I would not wake up my husband. I was really searching and really hurt by all that was going on. All of a sudden, I heard the audible voice of Jesus who simply said, 'Peggy, get your eyes on me.' That's all He said, He didn't have to say more. His voice was so compassionate, kind and loving. He could have been really stern with me, but He wasn't. I experienced an amazing peace and my hurt was gone. I finished out that year and then resigned. I learned an important lesson about obedience and the importance of following God's direction and listening to Him. I would have avoided a lot of heartache if I would have just heeded the Holy Spirit's direction and said 'no' to the job. But in the midst of it all, God allowed me to experience the most amazing reassurance from Him. God had mercy on me, because of His unfailing love and His great compassion. He was faithful even though I had gone my own way and not heeded the prompting from His spirit. He knew my heart and He loved me and would never leave me." ~ Peggy

THE FATHER, SON AND HOLY SPIRIT WILL ALWAYS ... BRING QUICK CONVICTION

God's conviction is a strong, clear and immediate inner knowing about whether to do something or not do something. His conviction is also felt when you need to change/correct something you have already done.

"There was a time in my life when I had been praying that God would help me see His Spirit at work. About that same time, I was on my way to Bible study when I noticed a lady walking along the side of the road. As I was passing her, God instructed me to stop and pick her up. Rather than stopping, I provided God with a host of reasons why it simply didn't make sense to do that, including the fact that I was on my way to *Bible study*. God spoke to me again. Although it wasn't in an audible voice it was *very* clear. He reminded me that I had been asking Him to help me see His Holy Spirit at work and said, 'Ok, I'm showing it to you, so why are you ignoring me? You have plenty of time, go back and pick her up.' This time I obeyed and as the woman got into my car I quickly made it abundantly clear that the *only* reason I was picking her up was because God told me to! 'I can't believe it,' she said, 'I was just praying that God would send someone to pick me up.' She explained that the bus had dropped her off at the wrong place and she was having difficulty walking because she had hurt her foot. I took her to her destination. We sat and talked for a while and I learned she had been raised in a Christian home, had gone through a season of rebellion and was just finding her way back to the Lord. I realize if I had not picked her up, someone else would have; but I would have missed that blessing! God had answered my prayer and given me the opportunity to see His Spirit at work." ~ Peggy

The correction and conviction of the Holy Spirit may be strong but it is *always* stated in positive terms. God may point out that an action or attitude is wrong, but He won't call you "stupid" or bombard you with thoughts of how useless and beyond hope you are. He will *never* offer you the thought that you are a failure and there is no use in trying.

When God's conviction comes as corrective action, failure to heed that correction can lead to His loving discipline.

> Those whom I [dearly and tenderly] love, I rebuke and discipline [showing them their faults and instructing them]; so be enthusiastic and repent [change your inner self—your old way of thinking, your sinful behavior—seek God's will]. Revelation 3:19 AMP

God's discipline is always done in love for the purpose of re-directing us.[18] Proverbs offers straightforward, repeated warnings for those who ignore God's discipline, along with some remarkable promises for those who heed His correction.

> I called you so often, but you wouldn't come. I reached out to you, but you paid no attention. You ignored my advice and rejected the correction I offered. So I will laugh when you are in trouble! I will mock you when disaster overtakes you— .... Proverbs 1:24-26 NLT

> Hear instruction, and grow wise; do not refuse it. Proverbs 8:33 CJB

> Poverty and disgrace come to those who ignore discipline, but the one who accepts correction will be honored. Proverbs 13:18 HCSB

> Anyone who ignores discipline despises himself, but whoever listens to correction acquires good sense. Proverbs 15:32 HCSB

THE FATHER, SON AND HOLY SPIRIT WILL ALWAYS ... FOSTER HUMILITY & FORGIVENESS

The Holy Spirit will always lead us to deny ourselves and glorify God. The entirety of the life as a Christ-follower is learning to die to self (Luke 9:23).

A common area in our life where God will ask us to humble ourselves is when we need to forgive an offense or ask for forgiveness for something we said or did. God won't say something like, *"Wow, you should feel really bad about what you said."* He will speak clearly so we know, for example, that a specific thing we said was not spoken with the right spirit and we need to ask for forgiveness.

While I was visiting a family member the next door neighbor came over to chat. Although God had instructed me several years ago that He wanted me to live by this principle: "Take no offense/Leave no offense" I made a comment to that neighbor that I could tell offended my family member. Early the next morning the Holy Spirit brought to my remembrance the conversation from the day before. He pointed out that what I had said (although factually true) was not said in an honoring way. I had left an offense and needed to ask for forgiveness. On issues of forgiveness, like everything else God commands, I have learned from experience that immediate obedience is always for our best. We will never have MORE grace than the grace available to us for immediate obedience!

THE FATHER, SON AND HOLY SPIRIT WILL ALWAYS ... BE SPECIFIC

Pastor Tom Holladay, Saddleback Church, calls God's voice "a pinpoint of light." Everything God says is relevant and important. "He doesn't engage in chitchat."[19] When He speaks, He speaks with conciseness and with precision. His goal is to communicate the objectives He has in mind and His desire is for us to be attentive to the specific things He says.

"I was in my own business for 11 years. During that time, I learned if I would consult the Lord for my business that it made the task of 'business,' so much easier. It started when I was about to make the biggest presentation of my business career to a VERY large account my business partner and I wanted to acquire. I had prepared a 17-page presentation with all of the numbers, features, advantages and benefits of our program. I was in the parking lot of the account and thought maybe I should pray before going in. After I had prayed the Lord surprisingly spoke to me! He told me to remove 11 pages from the presentation. I said, 'Lord, are you sure? Maybe I didn't hear you.' But He confirmed what He had said. So, I removed the pages and upon meeting the buyer I handed over my now much smaller presentation. I began with a brief conversation, now from the heart, and not from the numbers on why they should consider having our product in their stores. When I finished talking I could tell the buyer was thinking. I believe what was really happening was the Lord was speaking to his heart and mind. He looked up at me and said, 'you know, we should be in this business!' Of course, I agreed. Two weeks later I received a letter of approval. At one point this account was 48% of our business." ~ Bill

"I have found myself living by two words over the last few years. For example: "be available," "lean in," "confident expectation," "be intentional," "disciple others," "Jesus FIRST," "show up," "trust God," "let go," "Let God" and so on. ~ Colleen

God habitually provides Colleen with these short but specific two-word instructions and then she knows what to do. I would like to add a caveat here. God speaks very specifically, but we often don't understand until we are looking at His instruction in the rearview mirror!

In September, 2016 I was packing for a trip to Washington D.C. Derf and I were going to be a part of a 6-member prayer team there. We knew there would be a lot of walking. Although I am prone to blisters because of arthritis in my feet, in previous assignments I had been able to figure out a way to change shoes often enough to prevent them. Three times while I was packing for that September trip I heard the Holy Spirit tell me to "pack blister band aids." The first two times I dismissed His voice because I thought to myself I've already got this! But the third time I heard the instruction I decided I needed to heed it — although it still did not make sense to me. I even remember muttering under my breath, "I'm not sure what these are for Holy Spirit but I'll pack them!" On the third morning in D.C., one of the women texted me from her hotel room that she had rubbed two very large and painful blisters on the bottom of her foot from the walking the day before. The Holy Spirit reminded me that I had packed a few blister band aids and I should offer them to her. As I was packing God's voice was very specific, but I did not understand until the need arose why He instructed me to pack those band aids. They weren't for me; they were for another team member. You can bet I was very glad I obeyed His instruction. Those band aids enabled her to do the walking she needed to do that day. The words were clear and specific, but it was only in hindsight that I had understanding.

My second example comes from the same D.C. trip. As I was praying about preparation for that trip the Holy Spirit clearly said, "take your travel Bible you will have need of it." I always travel with a Bible so I inquired about the need and understood I needed to give it away. I had looked long and hard for a travel Bible that met all my requirements and I thought to myself, I hope this is easy to replace after I give it away. There was a time when the 6 members of the team came together to pray; I had my travel Bible sitting on the table in front of me. After we finished our time of prayer, one of the women asked where I had purchased the elastic bands that kept the pages of my Bible firmly together. I told her I had made them and I offered to make her a set and mail them to her since she lives in another state. It was THEN that the Holy Spirit prompted me to give her the set of bands that were on my Bible and make a new set for me. Now I understood His instruction — I needed to take my travel Bible which had those elastic bands because God wanted to bless her. I had heard God's specific instruction and had obeyed, but only in hindsight did I fully understand the instruction. It sounded like one thing, but in reality, it was different than I thought.

THE FATHER, SON AND HOLY SPIRIT WILL ALWAYS ... FOCUS ON HOW & WHY

As a part of helping you grow and mature, Holy Spirit will point out *"why"* and *"how"* an action you took or something you said was inconsistent with God's Word. The Spirit will bring to your understanding how to take a different action or say what you said differently.

"One day I was speaking to my boss about a situation and intentionally used a pretty coarse curse word. It had not been a part of my language for a very long time, but there was something strangely satisfying and empowering about using it that day. God, on the other hand, had a very different opinion! Shortly after that word came out of my mouth I heard the conviction of the Holy Spirit. His message was short and to the point. He told me *that* language is not who I am and that I was able to choose better words! I was instructed not to use the word again. In addition, He clearly asked me to return to my boss immediately and apologize. I quickly did what the Holy Spirit convicted me to do and as soon as I responded to His discipline the matter was dropped. There was no condemnation, there was no feeling bad, no shame — I simply felt corrected and it was over." ~ Rhonda

The conviction Rhonda experienced is entirely consistent with God's Word. See for example:

No foul language is to come from your mouth, but only what is good for building up someone in need, so that it gives grace to those who hear. Ephesians 4:29 HCSB

Coarse and foolish talking or crude joking are not
suitable, but rather giving thanks. Ephesians 5:4 HCSB

THE FATHER, SON AND HOLY SPIRIT WILL ALWAYS ... BRING PEACE & CLARITY

The voice of God is calm, quiet and confident. What God has spoken to you may look difficult, dangerous or impossible. Even if that's true, it is possible to have a peace that is beyond our own understanding. This is the very peace Jesus told His disciples He was giving them (John 14:27). Along with peace, expect God's voice to be clear. He may not give you all the details, but what He does speak will be understandable. Satan, on the other hand, is a master of anxiety and confusion.

THE FATHER, SON AND HOLY SPIRIT WILL ALWAYS ... ENCOURAGE JOYFULNESS

Joy acknowledges the goodness of God and is a source of spiritual strength. God knows that choosing joy in the midst of every circumstance is for our best. His nudges, His voice will *always* encourage us to refrain from complaint and discontentment. The truth is that when we walk in a spirit of dissatisfaction, irritation or displeasure with our circumstances we lose joy. The very nature of biblical joy is that it "flows from contentment of the heart regardless of the occasion."[20] Therefore, it is impossible for joy to co-exist with disapproval of God's plan. Moreover, a spirit of complaint forfeits God's grace which would have equipped, empowered and enabled us to glorify God in the midst of those very circumstances. Philippians 4:4-8 provides a very practical way for us to avoid Satan's trap to sabotage our joy.

In the next chapter we will turn our attention to clues which help us identify Satan's voice. In preparation for that subject matter, I want to share an experience to help us understand why correctly identifying the voice we are listening to matters.

I have unwittingly been held captive in a war I did not realize I was in! Let me explain. God gave me an assignment I agreed to do even though I really did not want to do it. That set up the perfect opportunity for Satan to oppose God's plan. Satan immediately began to feed me a steady stream of subtle lies that were offered so craftily that I failed to recognize him at work. Because I did not correctly identify the true source of those lies I resisted God and what He had planned for my best. All the while I should have been taking those thoughts captive and fighting against Satan! After two years, God's revelation came suddenly and I realized I had been battling God as if *He* was my enemy when all that time I should have been fighting Satan head on, lie by lie!

CHAPTER 8

SATAN'S VOICE

A S WE SAW in our last Chapter there are some very distinguishing attributes associated with God's voice. Those characteristics are so consistent we could call them "rules of recognition." As we have noted, Satan's voice is characteristically different than God's voice. This Chapter will identify some "rules of recognition" as it relates to the voice of our enemy.

Before we begin, let me note here that as I have taught this study I have encountered occasional objections to this type of focus on the enemy's voice. That opposition seems to be rooted in the firm belief held in some Christian circles that because the enemy of our souls is a defeated foe, we should not give him even so much as the time of day. In other words, it has been taught that we should pay no attention to the devil or give him any credit whatsoever. Please understand I am not teaching that we should ever give more credit to the enemy than to our God! Nor am I suggesting we carry on a conversation with Satan. On the other hand, I do believe it is biblically sound that we recognize we are in a spiritual war. We have an enemy who is always at work and we should not be unaware of the strategies he uses against us because we are disciples of Christ. Let's consider just a few Scriptures which make this clear:

Be of sober *spirit*, be on the alert. Your adversary, the devil, prowls around like a roaring lion, seeking someone to devour. 1 Peter 5:8

Submit therefore to God. Resist the devil and he will flee from you. James 4:7

I [Paul] have done this so we may not be taken advantage of by Satan. For we are not ignorant of his schemes. 2 Corinthians 2:11 HCSB

In each case, these words were written to Christ-followers as instruction in the ordinary course of life.

My husband has been working diligently to rid our yard of squirrels which are damaging the grass. He purchased some traps and is daily doing catch and release to another location with plenty of acorn-ladened oak trees. One morning there was a surprise in the cage, it was a large racoon who had literally stuffed himself inside in order to eat the bait. To make matters worse, he had pulled nearby palm fronds into the cage with him making the inside even more compact. If you can picture that in your mind's eye you are visualizing a good picture of what the enemy's plan is for each Christ-follower. He wants to take us captive! Moreover, once he traps us he wants to keep us in captivity. The idea of being snared in a trap is actually a biblical picture of Satan's schemes! In Matthew 13:41-43, Jesus warned that:

The Son of Man will send out His angels, and they will gather from His kingdom everything that causes sin [*skandalon*] and those guilty of lawlessness. They will throw them into the blazing furnace where there will be weeping and gnashing of teeth. Then the righteous will shine like the sun in their Father's kingdom. Anyone who has ears should listen!

In Luke 17:1, Jesus also warned:

"It is inevitable that stumbling blocks [*skand-alon*] come, but woe to him through whom they come!
…"

As you can see, the word "sin" in Matthew's text and the phrase "stumbling block" in Luke 17 is the Greek noun *skandalon* {skan'-dal-on}. It is an ancient word used originally to describe the bait stick in a trap.[1] The hunter would place the bait on the stick in order to attract the prey. The bait stick is what triggered the trapping mechanism to capture the animal. Therefore, the word *skandalon* is a vivid metaphor for a trap, a stumbling block or enticement to sin.

A trap needs two things to be successful: 1) it must be hidden and 2) it must be baited. Bait that remains *in* the trap cannot harm us. It's when we take the bait Satan offers that we get caught in the trap he has set. Since his goal is to take us captive, it really doesn't matter to him what bait he uses — as long as it works!

It is important to be alert to the fact that Satan will often change the bait he uses if his first attempt to trap us was not successful. In other words, he will switch tactics without notice! For example: If he attempts to get us trapped in fear and we avoid that trap with *faith* he may quickly switch to offering *pride* that we handled the situation so well. But pride is simply his next tactic to ensnare us! The truth of the matter will be that we will only have escaped his trap because of God's grace. Therefore humility (dependence on God) is the correct response every time we defeat Satan.

Our enemy is devious and deceptive, but we can learn the sound of his voice. So, let's look at common characteristics of the voice of our enemy — telltale signs that the voice we are hearing is *his* deceptively misleading voice, not God's voice.

SATAN WILL … TYPICALLY START OUT SMALL

Satan will usually send out a *scout thought* to see if it is accepted.[2] (A scout is someone sent out to examine or observe for the purpose of obtaining information; like a soldier sent out ahead of the army to gather information about the position and strength of the enemy). If we don't take that first little thought captive and evaluate its true source, Satan will send a second scout thought. If that thought is received by his victim then he will keep adding thought after thought until the person is literally bombarded with Satan's voice and buried under a pile of enemy thoughts.

The image that comes to mind is a child who wants to walk on a frozen pond. If he is wise, he tests the pond first by gingerly stepping out onto the ice along an edge. If that ice holds his weight, the child will carefully work his way forward on the frozen surface, usually sending out one foot ahead of the other, retaining the bulk of his weight on the stationary foot. When the ice on his extended foot holds the weight applied, he carefully brings his stationary foot forward to meet that extended foot. In this way, each step is a test step (or we could say a "scout step") that takes him deeper onto the surface of the ice until he has reached his goal.

Satan Will ... Lie and Distort the Truth

The enemy is *persistently* at work distorting truth and breathing out lies. Jesus called Satan the father of lies and said lying was his native language (John 8:44). There is no truth in him. I wonder if God removed his ability to speak truth when he fell from his position as the lead worship angel?[3] I wonder if that was done for our protection!

One of the ways Satan lies is through exaggeration. He exaggerates how difficult a God-given assignment might be. He embellishes a small irritation until we are convinced it is a big one. He exaggerates the adverse consequences of our obedience to something God has asked us to do. Satan majors in the "what-ifs" always amplifying and overstating the worst-case scenario!

Another way Satan deceives Christ-followers is to disguise himself as an angel of light (2 Corinthians 11:14). He cannot really transform himself into a true angelic messenger, but he certainly can masquerade in a most deceptive way.

As we have previously learned, Jesus made it very clear that because His sheep *know His voice* they will *not* follow the voice of a stranger (John 10:1-5). Again, sheep naturally recognize and follow their own shepherd, whereas it is unnatural for them to follow a stranger.[4]

SATAN WILL ... LEAD YOU TO JUSTIFY YOUR WORDS & ACTIONS

After you sin, Satan will encourage you to justify what you did or said. Satan fosters pride; he never wants you to admit you were wrong and ask for forgiveness. He will offer you thoughts which justify the action you have taken or the words you spoke. He will also tempt you to use methods to accomplish God's will that do not honor God, then excuse the means as unimportant as long as the result was obtained.

Let's return for a moment to the testimony I shared about the offensive remark I made when talking to my family member's neighbor. When the Holy Spirit brought conviction about the attitude of my heart at the time I made that remark, I started to defend myself to God. I began justifying my remark as being factually true and therefore warranted. It didn't take me long before I recognized that my justification was actually evidencing my heart's rebellion at that moment. In my pride, I did not want to apologize! Thankfully I came into agreement with Holy Spirit and did what He had instructed me to do. My husband has a standing rule of thumb by which he operates. He says it this way, "as soon as I begin to justify my actions in my thoughts I am already walking in sin."

SATAN WILL ... CONFUSE

Confusion prevents us from being able to connect all the dots. It is disorienting and leads to fear. Fear is a loss of courage and the eventual result is that we become paralyzed.[5]

The truth is God is *not* the God of disorder (1 Corinthians 14:33). On the other hand, Satan is a master at doubt and confusion! He will toss out all kinds of half-truths, partial proposals and a host of conflicting statements. His goal is to distract, distort and confuse. Through repeated accusations he wants you to feel helpless, stuck in self-doubt and unable to move.

Because God is a God of order we can pray and ask God to help us discern truth from lies and bring order out of chaos. As we pray, we can have confident expectation God *will* answer.

SATAN WILL ... OFFER A SHORTCUT

Satan will tempt you to stop short of fully obeying what God has instructed you to do. He will seek to convince you that God will still be pleased with half-hearted, half-finished obedience.

The book of first Samuel records one of the clearest examples in the Bible of God's reaction to partial obedience. King Saul was commanded to destroy the Amalekites and every possession they had. Because Saul spared the Amalekite king and "some" of the sheep, oxen and choicest things from the spoils, Samuel delivered this word of the Lord to Saul: "… Rebellion is as sinful as witchcraft, and stubbornness as bad as worshiping idols. So, because you have rejected the command of the LORD, he has rejected you as king."[6] God's opinion of partial obedience has never changed!

SATAN WILL ... CAUSE YOUR HEART TO BECOME CALLOUSED

Satan's accusations will make you overreact. He will egg you on to retaliate and get even no matter how slight the offense. A calloused heart will say things like: "Who cares!" "I give up anyway!" "Why try?" "Whatever!" Your goal in life will become selfish self-centered protection. You'll go from healthy boundaries to a high walled fortress protecting you from *all* emotions — not just bad emotions, but good emotions too. When your defensive walls go up, everyone and everything will be kept at bay, not just the people you want to avoid, but *everyone* (including God). Satan's trap is to try to isolate you!

SATAN WILL ... CONNIVE YOU INTO OVER-COMPENSATION

Satan will bombard you with persistent thoughts until you take responsibility that doesn't belong to you. He will whisper lies to you until you feel indispensable, irreplaceable and like a lone ranger. You'll hear yourself saying, "I'm the only one! If I don't do it, no one will!" You'll fall headlong into the martyr role. You will find various ways to show everyone *you* are the one doing *all* the work. You'll proclaim martyrdom to anyone who will listen. "I was the only one here last night. I stayed until 4 a.m. I only had enough time to shower and change; I didn't get any sleep." On the other hand, Jesus said: "So you too, when you do all the things which are commanded you, say, 'We are unworthy slaves; we have done *only* that which we ought to have done (Luke 17:10, italics in original).'"

SATAN WILL ... ACCUSE & CONDEMN

Satan is called "the accuser of our brethren [who] has been thrown down, he who accuses them before our God day and night (Revelation 12:10)." The Greek word for "accuser" in Revelation 12:10 is *kategoros* {kat-ay'-gor-os}. It is a noun that derives from the verb *kategoreo* meaning to charge with an offense; accuse mainly in a legal setting such as before a judge.[7] As a noun, *kategoros* refers to one who speaks against another openly in the sense of condemning or accusing. The opposite would be to speak well of, to bless.[8] Satan will repeatedly accuse us and replay the accusations over and over until we feel rebuked, worthless and condemned. Satan will first tempt us and then he will tattle on us.

I recently experienced the enemy's accusation following a phone call with a fellow Christ-follower. That individual firmly believed God had told him that I should join a certain non-profit organization to help them make decisions. However, when my husband and I prayed about the matter we both understood God's answer to be "no, I was not to join that organization." The individual graciously received my answer, but after the phone call concluded, I was repeatedly accused in my thoughts that I had gotten it all wrong. After a short time had elapsed I recognized the condemnation I was experiencing and let it go, recognizing the source of the lie. As a matter of fact, Satan's accusation actually confirmed for me that I had gotten it right!

Again, using language from a courtroom setting,[9] the Bible makes clear that "there is now **no** condemnation for those who are in Christ Jesus (Romans 8:1, bold added)."

"I gave my heart to Jesus and was baptized when I was about 9 years old; however, at about 12 years old I allowed the enemy to lead me into activity I should never have been doing. I would go to church, take an empty seat and watch the clock waiting impatiently to get out of there, yet was quick to boast of how much of a Christian I was. When I joined the military, I was getting to know God again during my deployments because He was all I had to save me in times of desperation. Once I returned from deployment, I would go back to living life on my own terms putting God in my back pocket until I needed Him again. After numerous failed relationships I gave up looking for a wife and started the process of repentance a little bit. It was then that God put an angel right in front of me. Her name was Allison [not her real name]. We took to each other quickly but we were not honoring God in our lives. Quite a few times, I would find myself going to church alone and sitting alone. Allison was slowing growing in her faith, but it wasn't a priority by any means. Then our church began a 'small group' and we began to study God's Word with others. As we did, God's Word convicted us of our sin and we both decided we wanted to start doing things the right way! I asked Allison to marry me and thanked God for all He had done for me. During this time, I felt it was important to start attending men's small groups. I was able to form close bonds with men who were also on fire for Christ. They taught me about obedience, tithing and learning about true fruits and blessings from God above. As we allowed iron to continue to sharpen iron, God was really working in our lives. We found ourselves giving more, being responsible for more, and on top of all of it, being blessed abundantly way more than we were giving. In the process we rededicated our lives to God giving it all to Him. We learned the sound of God's voice and found Him speaking to us in multiple ways. We heard Him speak through music, through other people, through co-workers and He also spoke to our spirits telling us that others need us. Because of the courage He gave us we were privileged to be part of the prayer team located at the front lines of the battle-field at a Freedom Retreat. We prayed for freedom for over 300 people who showed up with the same exact shameful ties we had had at one time in our lives. These people were not living in freedom but we were going to show them the way! As I write this at my work desk, I look at my Bible sitting right here in front of me out in the open and I realize *this* was the path God has had for me all along. I am living proof that He is oh so very, very good." ~ Johnny (not his real name)

Johnny's testimony is a good illustration of how God does things when we turn to Him in obedience — there is now therefore NO CONDEMNATION (no guilty verdict) for anyone who is *in* Christ Jesus! "In Christ God condemns sin and we are free!"[10]

However, that doesn't stop the enemy of our souls from trying to harass us so we don't live in the freedom we actually have! Con-demnation is that nagging, gnawing feeling that you don't measure up and you *never* will. Conviction comes from God to correct us; condemnation comes from Satan to criticize. God's conviction flows out of His love for us; condemnation is motivated by Satan's hatred for God and everyone who is in covenant relationship with Him.

With some practice, it is easy to tell the difference between conviction (source: Holy Spirit) and condemnation (source: Satan). One tell-tale sign is to tune in to the prevailing thoughts and ac-tions that flow from the voice you are hearing. Conviction will lead your heart toward repentance and a desire to change your actions. On the other hand, condemnation will lead to despair — a sense of being trapped in a cycle of failure that you can't change.[11]

Condemnation and conviction both highlight the fact that you missed the mark; however, conviction points you to the solution while condemnation avoids the solution altogether and points a finger at YOU. Condemnation repeatedly points out what a failure you are and how badly you've messed up. On the other hand, conviction is the loving invitation of Jesus calling, "Come to Me, my desire is to forgive you!" The moment your heart responds to God's conviction and you confess your failure seeking to change, you will no longer feel conviction. It has accomplished its purpose. That's God's grace. On the other hand, condemnation is Satan's strategy to make you feel worse and worse.

A common area Satan will bring accusation in our life is sin we have already confessed to God. ALL accusations regarding sin we have previously confessed and repented of comes from Satan![12] The truth is, "If we confess our sins, He is faithful and righteous, so that He will forgive us our sins and cleanse us from all unrighteousness (1 John 1:9)."

Over the years God has taught me an effective way to handle Satan's accusation regarding past sin which has been confessed and forgiven by God. When the enemy offers an instant replay of a past sin complete with remorse, regret and condemnation, I agree with Satan that the sin he is pointing out was harmful. But I don't stop there. I praise God for His amazing grace and abounding love that when I confessed and repented of that sin He forgave me! I have found that rejoicing in the work of the cross is the best way to shut down the enemy's accusing taunt!

SATAN WILL ... OFFER SHAME

Satan does not play fair. He will tempt us with sin and when we have committed that sin he will offer shame to trap us in destructive emotions. The dictionary defines shame as "a painful feeling of humiliation or distress caused by the consciousness of wrong or foolish behavior."[13] "Shame is the most disturbing experience individuals ever have about themselves; no other emotion feels more deeply disturbing because in the moment of shame the self feels wounded from within."[14]

A clinical psychologist points out one of the most troubling aspects of shame: "Where we will likely have an urge to admit guilt, or talk with others about a situation that left us with guilty feelings, it is much less likely that we will broadcast our shame. In fact, we'll most likely conceal what we feel because shame does not make a distinction between an action and the self. Therefore, with shame, bad behavior is not separate from a bad self as it is with guilt."[15] The fact that feelings of shame usually prevent us from talking with others about the matter at hand is the very thing Satan uses to his advantage! Our self-imposed silence will keep us trapped in self-destructive secrecy.

In all things Jesus is our model. The author of Hebrews tells us that when Jesus went to the cross, He "despised the shame (Hebrews 12:2)." Crucifixion was purposefully reserved for slaves and criminals and intentionally consisted of "a perverse mix of humiliation and torture."[16] Yet Jesus made the choice to endure the cross "*despising* its shame." This is an amazing choice of words. The Greek word is *kataphroneō* {kat-af-ron-eh'-o}; a compound word combining *kata* meaning "down, according to" and *phroneō* which refers to "regulating behavior from an inner mind-set."[17]

One who "despises" shame in a shame/honor culture (like that of the first century world in which Jesus lived) is one who actually *experiences* the societal shame. However, he sets his mind to disregard it, thus stripping that shame of its power to force him to conform to the societal behavioral norms. In other words, in a culture where shame would have been an extremely strong and powerful influencer of behavior Jesus made the choice to overlook the agonizing shame of the cross! He totally disregarded the shame heaped upon Him as He endured the cross, refusing to allow it to divert Him from perfect obedience to His Father. Jesus chose to suffer for His Father's honor/glory.

In her *Psalm 23* Bible study Jennifer Rothschild offers what she calls an "über-practical" way to deal with guilt and shame. She says each morning when she awakens she imagines that goodness and mercy are waiting at her bedroom door to follow her everywhere she goes that day. If she notices guilt and shame trying to attack her, she stops what she is doing and speaks the truth out loud: "Only, as in o-n-l-y, goodness and mercy will follow me today!"[18] She testifies that she's done it and it works.

SATAN WILL ... FOSTER DISCONTENTMENT & COMPLAINT

Satan will go beyond tempting us to feel dissatisfied with our present circumstances; he will attempt to trap us in a thought-cycle of irritation that will eventually explode into complaining words. He knows that complaint forfeits our peace, blocks God's grace and robs us of the joy that is otherwise available to us through that grace.

SATAN WILL ... OFFER FEAR

There is one more significant difference between God's voice and Satan's voice that I want to address before we move on to the next topic. Simply put: God's voice releases faith (faith as a noun) but Satan offers fear. Simply stated, fear is "the self-deception that you are about to be separated from the thing you most value."[19] Fear and faith are incompatible. Fear aligns itself with the kingdom of darkness while faith is the currency of God's Kingdom. The author of Hebrews warns that "without faith it is impossible to please [God] (Hebrews 11:6)."

Most of Satan's power is in his bluff. He knows that living in constant fear of disaster can be as disabling as the disaster itself.[20] It's not hard to imagine how fear comes to us. Satan subtly offers us a "'what if'" thought and if we don't take that thought captive and make it obedient to Christ, Satan will offer another fear-based thought. Before we know it, we can find ourselves smothered by a thick blanket of fear and wonder how we ever got there!

Because we don't want to get ensnared by Satan's fear trap, let's consider how we receive faith from God. First understand that in the Bible "faith" can be a noun or it can refer to an action. When God speaks a word of promise to us such as, "I will never leave you nor forsake you" the very words He speaks are truth. They are alive with power, promise and persuasion. If we choose to trust God and let those words find their home in our heart, faith (as a noun) begins to take root. Our actions (faith as a verb) will demonstrate that we are persuaded by the words God spoke and find them trustworthy enough to guide our thoughts and our behavior. Faith has the power to defeat fear. But the choice is always ours — we choose whose voice we will listen to — the voice that leads, or the voice that misleads.

The author of Hebrews tells us that we can train our ear to recognize the voice of God above all the noise. The mature are those "who because of practice have their senses trained to discern good and evil (Hebrews 5:14)." It is through repeated practice, by reason of regular and recurring use, that we are able to discern whether what we hear is of God or Satan.

In conclusion, we have discussed Satan's strategies as if they are singular and isolated, one from the other. Remember at the outset of this discussion we took note that he will change tactics any time he chooses and he does so without advance warning or notice.

One last thought: Jesus knows the thoughts that are in a man's heart (Matthew 9:4, 12:25). However, nowhere in Scripture are we ever told that Satan has the same ability to read our thoughts! Satan is an opportunist and he will be relentless until he finds a strategy that works to accomplish his objectives.

CHAPTER 9

ADDITIONAL INSIGHTS INTO GOD'S VOICE

W̲E WILL USE this Chapter to tidy up some loose ends. Our first topic is an important biblical reality about God's voice that we must accept although we likely won't understand *why* it is so. The fact is that our all-knowing God can speak about things in the future as though they are certain to happen, but then they don't. After exploring that biblical truth, we'll move on to practical steps we can take in order to better hear God's voice and conclude with the subject of fasting.

GOD CAN SPEAK OF POSSIBILITIES AS THOUGH THEY ARE REALITIES

Let's look at a time when David inquired of God and was told what Saul planned to do.

> One day news came to David that the Philistines were at Keilah stealing grain from the threshing floors. David asked the LORD, "Should I go and attack them?" "Yes, go and save Keilah," the LORD told him. But David's men said, "We're afraid .... We certainly don't want to go to Keilah to fight the whole Philistine army!" So David asked the LORD again, and again the LORD replied, "Go down to Keilah, for I will help you conquer the

Philistines." So David and his men went to Keilah. They slaughtered the Philistines and took all their livestock and rescued the people of Keilah .... Saul mobilized his entire army to march to Keilah and besiege David and his men. But David learned of Saul's plan and .... David prayed, **"O Lord, God of Israel, I have heard that Saul is planning to come and destroy Keilah because I am here. Will the leaders of Keilah betray me to him? And will Saul actually come as I have heard?** O Lord, God of Israel, please tell me." And **the Lord said, "He will come." Again David asked, "Will the leaders of Keilah betray me and my men to Saul?" And the Lord replied, "Yes, they will betray you.**" So David and his men ... left Keilah .... Word soon reached Saul that David had escaped, so he didn't go to Keilah after all .... Saul hunted him day after day, but God didn't let Saul find him. 1 Samuel 23:1-14 NLT, bold added

Notice when He answered David's questions about Saul's plans God spoke as if those plans were certain to occur. Even so, the things God told David *would* happen did not actually take place. Once David heard God's answers he and his men wisely left Keilah. When Saul heard that David was no longer in Keilah he abandoned his plan to go there.

Because God is omniscient, He foreknew the *possibility* of Saul's actions.[1] God created people with free will. He does not control the actions of people as though they are robots. David's change of plan led to Saul's change of plan so that in the end God's foreknowledge described a *possible* or *potential* event rather than an *actual* event. We might wonder why God would choose to speak about possibilities as though there were realities? God has taught me over a long season of hearing His voice that we are wise to refrain from trying to explain Him where He doesn't explain Himself.[2] Chuck Smith, founder of Calvary Chapel, acknowledges similar counsel he received from the Lord when he was mentally working overtime attempting to reconcile what appeared to him to be two irreconcilable truths of God's Word. He writes:[3]

> I said, "God, I can't understand it." It was then that the Lord spoke to my heart and said, "I didn't ask you to understand it, I only asked you to believe My Word."

What is important for the purposes of our study is that even though the events God spoke about did not happen, it was still God's voice that David heard. He knew it was God's voice and he acted on it.

PRACTICAL STEPS TO HEARING GOD'S VOICE

These practical steps to help you learn to hear God's voice are based on teaching by Pastor Robert Morris.[4] I have added comments based on my own experience.

1. Set an appointment to meet with God daily.

   a. Pick a time when you are at your best and select a meeting place that is well suited to your needs. Mark Batterson refers to that personal place where we can hear God a little louder and a little clearer as a "whispering spot."[5]
   b. People will often think "I don't have time to do this" but keep in mind we *always* make time for what we value.

   It occurs to me that God modeled this for us! He set appointments with Israel to meet with Him. (In Hebrew they are called *mo'ed* — appointed times; we know them as Sabbath and the Feasts commanded in Leviticus 23). Even on the first Passover in Egypt He set an appointment for the events of that night and at Sinai He set an appointment to meet with Israel on the third day.

2. Begin your meeting time with stillness and worship.

    a. Pastor Morris says he often worships by reading from
        the Psalms in the early morning hours. Sometimes
        he reads a Psalm a day until he has read all the way
        through and then he starts back at the beginning.
        Other times he simply asks God what Psalm he
        should read that morning and when God brings a
        number to his mind he reads from that Psalm. He
        said it is truly amazing how many times God will
        speak a word to him either in or from the particular
        Psalm Holy Spirit led him to.

        I concur wholeheartedly with his suggested approach.
        There are times when I *need* to hear from God
        (usually in the face of an overwhelming sense of fear
        or doubt offered by the enemy). At those times I will
        ask God where to read in the Psalms. When I hear
        a number, I turn there expecting Him to meet me
        there. I have found this to be virtually a fail-proof
        way to hear in the midst of intense need.

    b. Pastor Morris shares that he will often start his
        meeting time with God by asking Him what song
        He would like to hear from him that morning and
        when a song enters his thoughts he sings it silently
        in his mind to God.

3. Spend time reading God's Word and praying whatever is
    presently on your heart.

4. Listen attentively and write. Begin by writing what you
    think God is saying to you about the Scripture you just
    read. You may want to write out your prayers. Write down
    anything you believe God is impressing on your heart about
    your prayers. Write down questions which require God's
    wisdom and listen for His answers. I provide my own
    thoughts about the value of journaling in the last Chapter.

John Eldredge shares one way in which he allows God to initiate conversation. He comments that as his day or week progresses he turns his heart and thoughts toward God. At those times he stops and asks God what He is saying? Eldredge says this gives God an open opportunity to speak into whatever is presently happening in his life or to say whatever God might need to say to him at that moment.[6] And then he adds, God "knows the very words we need to hear. What he will say to me is exactly what my heart needs to hear, [they] will be the very words that best convey his meaning to my heart with greatest precision."[7]

Eldredge provides a number of easy to follow guidelines when you are seeking God's direction on a particular matter.[8]

1. Begin with small questions
2. Repeat the question quietly in your heart to God
3. If you don't seem to be able to hear God's voice immediately, Eldredge suggests you can "try on" possible answers. For example, "*Is it yes, you want us to go?*" Then pause and listen. If there is no answer, then "try on" another question, such as "*Or is it no, you want us to stay home?*" Pause and listen again.[9] Stopping long enough to listen is a vitally important part of hearing what God wants to say.
4. Be open as you listen. Sometimes God wants to speak to you about something entirely different than the question you're asking Him. If He doesn't seem to be answering the question you're asking, then ask Him what he *does* want to say.[10]
5. If God does provide direction about the matter, ask the *next* natural question. Eldredge advises, "so often we get an answer to the first part of a question but fail to ask the second half." He provides the following example, "We hear, '*Yes, take the job*,' or '*Yes, sell the house.*' Then we need to ask, '*When? Today, next week, next year?*' Don't just get a first impression and then blast ahead."[11]

Throughout this process it is important to remain alert to inner promptings. With experience there will be times when we can sense the answer even before God puts it into words. Our spirit is in union with the Spirit of God and He often reveals His will to us deep within before it forms into understandable words. Sometimes stillness gives the Holy Spirit the opportunity to put into words what He is saying; other times we need to follow up with straightforward questions and wait on His reply.

A WORD ABOUT FASTING

Generally biblical fasting refers to abstaining from food as a way of expressing "dependence on God and submission to His will."[12] Both Jesus (Matthew 4:1-2) and Moses (Exodus 34:28) fasted for 40 days. Fasting is directly connected to preparation for communicating with God in Exodus 34:28; Deuteronomy 9:9; and Daniel 9:3. Fasting is a form of denying the flesh something it desires and by doing so we put ourselves in a better position to hear God. Jesus directly addresses fasting in the New Testament.

> Then the disciples of John came to [Jesus], asking, "Why do we and the Pharisees fast, but Your disciples do not fast?" And Jesus said to them, "The attendants of the bridegroom cannot mourn as long as the bridegroom is with them, can they? But the days will come when the bridegroom is taken away from them, and then they will fast...." Matthew 9:14-15

Jesus taught His disciples:

> "Whenever you fast, do not put on a gloomy face as the hypocrites *do*, for they neglect their appearance so that they will be noticed by men when they are fasting. Truly I say to you, they have their reward in full. But you, when you fast, anoint your head and wash your face so that your fasting will not be noticed by men, but by your Father who is in secret; and your Father who sees *what*

is done in secret will reward you...." Matthew 6:16-18, italics in original

Fasting is not obligatory, but Jesus presumes His followers *will* fast after His death. His instruction is to fast in such a way that you don't call undue attention to yourself in the process. He clearly instructed His followers that their fast must come from the heart, be done in secret to God alone and not be done as an outward display to impress other people. His instruction suggests this is the only type of fasting that honors Him. In the same way, God rejected Israel's fasts when they were done with improper motive (Isaiah 58).

Fasting is between you and God; during fasting we keep our focus on the Lord and His will. The Bible makes plain that fasting and prayer regularly go together (Jeremiah 14:11-12; Nehemiah 1:4; Ezra 8:21, 23). We do not fast to manipulate God nor do we fast to earn anything from Him. God can disregard a fast motivated by a wrong purpose, no matter how well intended.

As I was writing this study, Rhonda, one of my sisters in Christ who fasts regularly, shared with me that she was watching a movie during a season in which she was fasting. Although the movie had nothing whatsoever to do with fasting, in the midst of that movie she heard God say, "you do not have to do this [referring to her fast] to earn my love." She was very surprised. She had never consciously thought of her fasting as an attempt to earn God's love but she realized that God saw the truth of the matter and gently assured her His love was always freely available to her!

When fasting is used as a strategy to hear God's voice, the purpose of fasting is to prepare *our* heart. A successful fast for the purpose of hearing God's voice, no matter the duration or the type, always results in a prepared heart.

There are degrees of fasting, both as to the time of abstinence from food, and whether the abstinence is total or partial. A fast may involve one specific food, a meal, or all food. On the other hand, a fast that positions us to better hear God's voice can involve pleasures other than food. For example, God may prompt you to forego shopping or movies or TV for a specified time period.

Recently our Sr. Pastor encouraged everyone to ask God what they should fast in preparation for a church-wide week of prayer. God decided to introduce me to a new type of fast! I was surprised when He told me to fast "fear." I had never thought of fasting in that way before. I'm almost a week into the fast and I can tell you it is a wonderful strategy for becoming aware of the ways in which enemy tries to offer me fear. Moreover, the fact that I've made a conscious decision to "fast" that emotion has emboldened me to stop Satan in his tracks the moment I realize he is offering fear.

"As a part of our ministry services I felt led to open *She Brews* a coffee house in the town where we operate our ministry homes for women recovering from drug addiction. She Brews is designed to employ these women as a part of their successful recovery program. Many months I find myself 'too short' in coffee house profits to make my payroll. When I don't know what else to do, I fast and seek God as to whether I am to close She Brews or keep it open. Invariably He will provide the money in one way or another so I can cover another payroll and I know I am to keep the coffee house open at least one more month." ~ Rhonda

CHAPTER 10

FINE TUNING

N O MATTER HOW experienced we are in hearing God's voice there are times when confirmation is vitally important to us and there will definitely be times when we risk getting it wrong. These important subjects are addressed in this Chapter along with some filters experienced ministers and Bible teachers use to help them discern God's voice.

SEEKING CONFIRMATION THAT YOU ARE HEARING GOD'S VOICE

One way in which God uses circumstances to speak to us is what Priscilla Shirer calls "the mercy of confirmation" which can assure us that we are hearing God's voice in a given matter. In other words, there are times when external circumstances can confirm what you think you are hearing.

"During the month of May 2008, I prayed in the Spirit each day in my car as I was driving back and forth to work. A month later to the day after I had started praying I looked at a house to purchase as our first women's ministry house and the owner gave me immediate possession that same day indicating the details of the closing would be worked out later. I sent out a few text messages and in the course of two days the house was entirely furnished, including a refrigerator stocked with food, linens on the 4 donated beds and pictures hanging on the walls. I took possession of the house on Friday, on Monday morning four women released by the courts moved into their new transition home. God was the only one who could make that happen! It was His very clear confirmation that I had understood His call to begin this new ministry. A year later a second house was offered to me — we now operate 8 ministry homes and are a model in the state of Oklahoma for successful Christ-centered drug recovery services." ~ Rhonda

Priscilla Shirer notes that this is not the *primary* means of hearing God's voice, but it can be a helpful confirmation. "Others," she says, "might dismiss these providential alignments with God's will as merely coincidental, but to the one who is listening they can be God's way of giving you a nod or a wink from Heaven."[1] While confirmation is a way to be sure you heard God correctly, Shirer points out that confirmation is not a guarantee that you won't face challenges when you begin to do what God has called you to do.

When our heart attitude is right, God permits us to test His Word. This is a subject worth spending some time to explore.

"When I needed confirmation that God was asking us to move 1100 miles away to Kansas, I asked God to provide me with clear confirmation so that I would be certain of His plan. Over the course of three consecutive days, God provided confirmation in three different ways. The first was a quarter from Kansas, the second confirmation came on the second day when I was talking to a professor at Ohio State University about where Nathan might find a job and the professor seemed to randomly comment that he had heard there were a lot of dairy farms in Kansas. The third confirmation came the next day when one of Nathan's relatives mentioned they were going to be traveling to Kansas. God had clearly provided confirmation by repeating references to 'Kansas' in very different and unexpected ways." ~ Kimberly

He allows us to "put out the fleece." When He speaks, God expects obedience. Scripture is certain that He permits us to take the time to ask for clarity or double-check what we think we have heard. However, God knows the difference between a search for clarity or confirmation and deliberate delay resulting from a rebellious heart. Judges 6 records Gideon's desire to be sure he had heard God correctly and illustrates God's willingness to be "tested" by a sincere heart.

You may recall the example of how God spoke through the pink rosebud at the end of Bible study one evening. I mentioned there was a second way He spoke clearly through one of those rosebuds. This second example is remarkably different than the first. On the very last day of class, the woman who received the rosebud had been contemplating whether she was correctly hearing God ask her to teach a women's Bible study. She told me that before class that day, God very specifically told her she would receive the rosebud in class *that* day and that when she did it would be His confirming sign that He had in fact called her to teach. She and I both marveled at how God used the rosebud that day to confirm His instruction to her.

One year towards the end of December the Lord spoke very clearly to me to indicate that my husband would be losing his job. Since I was already a full-time volunteer and no longer working for a salary it was hard to believe that I had heard God's voice clearly. Without sharing "what" God had said (in case I was wrong) I told my husband that the Lord had spoken some very unexpected things to me and that I needed to know for sure that I was hearing God's voice. We prayed together about my need for certainty and without telling me about it, my husband "put out a fleece" by asking God for a confirming sign. Later that same day when the "sign" he had asked for came to pass, he assured me that it was God's voice I had heard and indeed within a short number of days his company unexpectedly announced its first ever significant management downsizing — in spite of the fact that my husband was offered other positions to stay with his employer, we knew exactly what God's plan for him was and he knew how to respond.

It is important to understand that there is a difference between this type of *permissible testing* to confirm what you believe you have heard (for the purpose of obedience) and the trying or testing that Scripture warns against. In Matthew 4:7 and Luke 4:12 Jesus warns: "You shall not put the LORD your God to the test." The text makes plain that Jesus is referring to a warning Moses gave the people in Deuteronomy 6:16 "You shall not put the LORD your God to the test, as you tested *Him* at Massah."[2] The biblical narrative of what took place at Massah is recorded in Exodus 17:

> Then all the congregation of the sons of Israel jour-neyed by stages from the wilderness of Sin, according to the command of the LORD, and camped at Rephidim, and there was no water for the people to drink. Therefore the people quarreled with Moses and said, "Give us water that we may drink." And Moses said to them, "Why do you quarrel with me? Why do you test the LORD?" But the people thirsted there for water; and they grumbled against Moses and said, "Why, now, have you brought us up from Egypt, to kill us and our children and our livestock with thirst?" So Moses cried out to the LORD, saying, "What shall I do to this people? A little more and they will stone me." Then the LORD said to Moses, "Pass before the peo-ple and take with you some of the elders of Israel; and take in your hand your staff with which you struck the Nile, and go. Behold, I will stand before you there on the rock at Horeb; and you shall strike the rock, and water will come out of it, that the people may drink." And Moses did so in the sight of the elders of Israel. He named the place Massah and Meribah because of the quarrel of the sons of Israel, and because they tested the LORD, saying, "Is the LORD among us, or not?" Exodus 17:1-7

Let's take a little side trip here in order to learn what a *test* is from God's perspective; then we'll return to the test God has chosen for Israel at Meribah. The Greek word for "tempt" and "test" is the exact same word: *peirasmos* {pi-ras-mos'}. An unchangeable truth is that God tempts no one (James 1:13). *Peirasmos* is a morally neutral word which describes the act of putting one to the test and it also refers to the test itself.

Tests (trials) come (sent or allowed by God) in order to discover a person's nature or spiritual quality. Think of yourself as a tube of spiritual toothpaste. Pressure (tests ~ temptations) simply brings out what is hidden on the inside (your character)! What is there is seen and known by God, but often it remains hidden to us unless something causes it to bubble up and out of us.

Since a Christ-follower has a new heart and God's indwelling Spirit, they can make a choice as to how they respond to the test/temptation. A test/temptation faced in a way that seeks to please our Father is valuable and beneficial to our spiritual growth (James 1:2,12). However, when we meet that same test with a wrong response, it becomes a temptation to evil. In other words, every trial/test will either end in the worship of God or the worship of the kingdom of darkness. The choice belongs to us!

Now that we understand how test/temptation works in God's Kingdom, let's return to the exodus story in order to understand why the test at Rephidim is called an impermissible testing of God. Each move Israel made in the wilderness was God-led as they followed the daytime cloud pillar and the nighttime fire pillar (Exodus 13:21-22). So, we see that it was *God* who led Israel to Rephidim where there was no water. In other words, it was God's will for them to face this dilemma. By His divine design He had chosen to test the response of the Israelites to adversity, in this case lack of water.[3]

By this time in their wilderness journey Israel should have learned to trust God to supply all their needs. He had provided water at Marah (Exodus 15:22-26) as well as quail and manna in the wilderness (Exodus 16). God was testing them for their own good. It was His purpose for them to see the rebellious condition of their hearts so they could realign their hearts according to the truth of His blessing and provision. In His sovereignty God has every right to test us and His tests are *always* for our good (Deuteronomy 8:16). As we have already learned, how we respond will determine whether the test is a blessing to us (in that we see our sinful heart condition and change our behavior) or whether it is simply a harsh test which tempts us to focus on our perceived lack.

On the other hand, no one has the right to "put God to the test." At Rephidim Israel was actually demanding that God do things *their* way, on *their* time table. Such testing essentially says, "I will trust *if* God proves Himself trustworthy and to be 'trustworthy' in my eyes God must prove Himself in the precise way I want Him to." Such defiant heart attitudes do not honor God and He warns against them. When we demand that God prove Himself trustworthy in this manner, it reveals a hardened, unbelieving heart.

The situation is entirely different when God suggests we test Him. He may invite us to put out the fleece. Biblical examples of God's invitation to test Him include:

Malachi 3:10 - "… Bring the whole tithe into the storehouse, so that there may be food in My house, and test Me now in this," says the LORD of hosts, "if I will not open for you the windows of heaven and pour out for you a blessing until it overflows.…"

Isaiah 7:11 where God spoke to King Ahaz inviting him to: "Ask a sign for yourself from the LORD your God; make it deep as Sheol or high as heaven."

Allow me to provide an example from my own experience: Several years ago, I was asked to serve on an organization's Board of Directors, but I did not believe it was an assignment the Lord had for me. There was some insistence from the person who extended the invitation so I agreed I would pray about it. When Derf and I sat down to pray, Derf said, "the Lord said that you are to put out a fleece." "Are you sure?" I asked. "You are the one who usually puts out the fleece, that's not how I hear answers from the Lord." Later that day I followed the direction my husband had given me;

I chose something I thought not likely to occur. Within minutes after my prayer, God provided the very sign I had asked to be a sign of confirmation. He obviously wanted me to be very certain that He was giving me an assignment to join that Board for a season.

WHAT IF I GET IT WRONG?

Henry Blackaby (author of *Hearing God's Voice* and *Experiencing God*) says that the only way he knows *for sure* that he correctly understood God's voice is when he looks back and sees he got it right![4] There is biblical support for Blackaby's rear-view-mirror approach. When Moses wanted confirmation that he had correctly understood God's direction to go back to Egypt and confront Pharaoh for the release of the Hebrew people, God's answer was that the confirming sign would be given to Moses *after* he had done what God instructed him to do.

> "Therefore, come now, and I will send you to Pharaoh, so that you may bring My people, the sons of Israel, out of Egypt." But Moses said to God, "Who am I, that I should go to Pharaoh, and that I should bring the sons of Israel out of Egypt?" And He said, "Certainly I will be with you, and this shall be the sign to you that it is I who have sent you: **when you have brought the people out of Egypt**, you shall worship God at this mountain."
> Exodus 3:10-12, bold added

In other words, Moses had to risk that he got it wrong before he had full assurance that he got it right! When trying to learn to hear God's voice it is important to relax and accept the reality that it is likely we will never totally and completely master discerning the voice of God in this present life. The good news is that when our hearts are centered on God's will, He always has a safety net in hand!

God commands us to "be perfect, as your heavenly Father is perfect."[5] However, perfection refers much more to meeting the goals God sets for us than being flawless in the ordinary sense of that word. In our western worldview attaining perfection means being faultless, having no room for improvement of any kind. On the other hand, biblically speaking if anything has fully attained the purpose for which God has designed it, it is perfect (Greek word *teleios*, from *telos* meaning goal, purpose). Therefore, the command to "be perfect" is a command to reach the goals God has set for us through "single-minded or wholehearted commitment to God's will."[6] While we are practicing we don't need to fear getting it wrong!

- ✓ God promises that He will never leave us, nor forsake us (Deuteronomy 31:6; Hebrews 13:5)
- ✓ No one can snatch us out of His hand (John 10:28-30)
- ✓ He hears the righteous when they call to Him for help (Psalm 34:17; Proverbs 15:29)
- ✓ He guides in a straight path. If we begin to stumble He promises to pick us up (Proverbs 4:11; Psalm 23:3; Psalm 37:24)

Given these biblical truths from a God who never changes, we can conclude that fear of getting it wrong is a tool Satan uses to prevent our obedience. Remember, each of these promises are given to us in seed form, they contain God's power of persuasion and He invites us to incubate them in our heart until they bear fruit. You may recall from our earlier discussion that this is true biblical faith — truth that finds its home in our heart!

Thanks be to God that grace not only covers sin, grace also covers our mistakes.[7] That means there is enough grace to handle every time we thought we understood God's voice and we missed it. Like every other area in our life where we miss the mark, when we confess and repent, we receive God's gracious forgiveness and then keep going. In God's hands our mistakes can become the fertile soil for future learning opportunities. That's grace!

FILTERS WHICH CAN HELP US DISCERN GOD'S VOICE

Some Christian ministers/teachers use filters of various types to help them discern God's voice. For example, Priscilla Shirer identifies the following "Five M's of Correctly Hearing God."[8]

1. Listen for Holy Spirit's message
2. Live in prayer mode — submit what you think you are hearing back to God in prayer
3. Search the model of Scripture. What does the Scripture have to say about the matter? Be careful not to simply pull out one Scripture and apply it, instead look for what Shirer calls "the Divine Highlighter in Scripture" meaning you read with the expectation that Holy Spirit will illumine the Scripture
4. Submit to a mature Christ-follower asking them to help you discern
5. Expect the "mercy of confirmation" when you ask God to verify what you think He is asking you to do

   We addressed the subject earlier when we talked about God speaking through other people. You may find it helpful to review that section of the study, in particular keeping in mind that "border bullies" are real people who can add more confusion than clarity; but "border buddies" and "border busters" can be invaluable aids to correctly and clearly hear God's voice.

I would add these two additional filters:

6. Dr. Shane T. Wood, Professor at Ozark Christian College, advises his students that when God provides direction for their life it will generally line up with how He has wired them.[9]

   This does not mean that God will only ask us to do things within our comfort zone. The fact is God will *often* ask us to do things that stretch us in one way or another. Lysa TerKeurst teaches that one of her filters to ascertain whether it is God speaking to her is whether the instruction she receives is "beyond herself." By that she means it is something that is "out of the ordinary" for her.[10]

In everything God gives us to do, His primary objective is to be glorified. One of the best ways for Him to get all the glory is to ask us to do something that may seem beyond our ability to do.[11] When we do what He asked, we only did it through the Holy Spirit (who enables all obedience). In that way, we can't help testifying about the truth — that He did what we could not do ourselves! Our testimony then glorifies Him. I think of it this way, when God gives us an assignment that is beyond us, He is setting us up for a testimony as we do what pleases Him (something our flesh is incapable of doing).[12]

Pastor Dave Folkerts, Calvary Chapel Melbourne, points out that when God does direct a dramatic turn in your life, He typically affirms it through several sources, in a variety of different ways. In his experience God's voice always goes in the same direction and gets a little stronger as time goes on when you are in the midst of a significant life change.

7.   Does what you are hearing line up with God's character and Godly wisdom?

It is important to note however that there is a difference between the wisdom of the world and God's wisdom. James tells us that God's "wisdom from above is first of all pure. It is also peace loving, gentle at all times, and willing to yield to others. It is full of mercy and the fruit of good deeds. It shows no favoritism and is always sincere (James 3:17 NLT)." Also keep in mind, as we have previously discussed, sometimes God will ask us to obey in ways that do not seem wise initially and only make sense to us in hindsight.

CHAPTER 11

GROWING MORE CONFIDENT

I HAVE WRITTEN this study from a very practical perspective. In this last Chapter you will find some very pragmatic suggestions about steps you can take if you don't believe you are hearing God's voice or if you simply want to increase the frequency with which you do. Because journaling has played such an important role in my own experience of hearing God speak, I've given it attention as its own topic and it too will be addressed in this final Chapter.

WHAT TO DO IF YOU ARE NOT HEARING FROM GOD

Begin by praying and asking God to help you increase your ability to hear Him. I often tell people who become anxious about hearing God's voice that He wants to speak to us even more than we want to hear Him. If we are listening, we can be confident He *will* find a way to speak to us!

Ask God to reveal to you anything that is hindering your ability to hear, including sin. Any pattern of sin in our life compromises our communication with God.

Sin such as a judging and/or complaining spirit or unforgiveness can block revelation from God.

During our first summer in Florida, the June heat and humidity was unusually high. We didn't know that and I began to wonder how we would handle August which everyone had warned us about as the absolute worst month for heat and humidity. One morning while we were traveling to Washington D.C. and we were just north of the Smoky Mountains with its beautiful fresh air, I was thanking God for morning temperatures that were more familiar to me. Then I asked God how will we ever be able to handle the heat and humidity of August? God clearly said to me: "You can complain or you can receive my grace, but you can't do both!" I immediately set my heart to refrain from having a complaining spirit so that I could freely receive His grace.

Practice being still more often. Reduce the speed with which you live your life and reduce the noise/distraction that surrounds you as you do. Lysa TerKeurst suggests that if you want God's voice to be the loudest voice in your life, ask Him what in your life needs to have the volume turned down?[1]

Increase the amount of time you spend in God's word. As we have noted, He often uses Scripture to speak.

If you still find yourself unable to hear God's voice, go back to the last time God spoke to you; ask yourself whether you fully obeyed. Why would God speak something new to you if you have not done what He previously spoke to you? I think this is one of the most important aspects of hearing God.

Robert Morris notes that when we disobey God, we leave His presence.[2] God has three types of presence in the life of a Christ-follower: His *omnipresence* (the fact that He is everywhere); His *manifest* (made known) presence and His *inner* presence (indwelling presence of Holy Spirit).[3] It is impossible to leave His *omnipresence* (Psalm 139:7-12). In our disobedience, we disrupt God's *inner* presence and leave His *manifest* presence. We need to confess and repent of that sin so we can be fully restored to His presence again.

The story of Jonah is an excellent illustration of this principle.

> The word of the LORD came to Jonah the son of
> Amittai, saying, "Arise, go to Nineveh, the great city, and
> cry out against it, because their wickedness has come up
> before Me." But Jonah got up to flee to Tarshish from the
> presence of the LORD. So he went down to Joppa, found a
> ship that was going to Tarshish, paid the fare, and boarded
> it to go with them to Tarshish away from the presence of
> the LORD. Jonah 1:1-3

The voice of God came to Jonah with a commission. Jonah left God's *manifest* presence and disrupted God's *inner* presence (the anointing he had as God's prophet) when he chose not to listen.[4] But in His *omnipresence* God still knew where Jonah was, so He spoke to Jonah with circumstances (i.e., the storm, the great fish — Jonah 1:4-17). When Jonah repented (Jonah 2:1-9), then God changed his circumstances (the great fish spit him out onto dry land — Jonah 2:10) and Jonah agreed and was enabled to do what God had commanded him to do. Notice that Jonah did not hear God speak again until he obeyed God's first instruction (Jonah 3:1). Jesus taught a similar principle:

> Then [Jesus] said to them, "Take heed what you hear.
> With the same measure you use, it will be measured to
> you; and to you who hear, more will be given...." Mark
> 4:24 NKJV

> "... Therefore take heed how you hear. For whoever
> has, to him *more* will be given; and whoever does not
> have, even what he seems to have will be taken from him."
> Luke 8:18 NKJV, italics in original

In Mark 4:24 and Luke 8:18 the word "heed" is a translation of the Greek word *blepo* which suggests physical sight but spiritual comprehension.[5] The word frequently implies intentional, earnest "contemplation (e.g., often in the sense of "keep your eyes open," or "beware")."[6] As used in the above quoted verses, *blepo* is a command which calls for continual close attention — when God speaks we are to pay attention!

It is a Kingdom principle that you will get more words from God if you will just act on the ones you get. If you don't, even what you seem to have can be taken away from you.

JOURNALING AS A TOOL

A tool I have found very helpful to hearing and discerning God's voice is journaling. For many women, this may bring back memories of a Diary we kept as young girls. This is *not* the type of journaling I'm talking about. It is not simply a written record of "what I did today." Here are some examples of how I have used journaling:

Journaling can be used to record lessons we know God is teaching us (for example those repetitions of Scripture that He provides when He wants to draw our attention to it). I sometimes start a journal by recording what I know to be true and find that God then fills in the blanks with greater understanding.

I have journaled questions I have for God and sometimes He brings an answer at that same time as I am journaling or delays the answer and it comes later in the day or on another day — even weeks or months later.

When I am feeling oppressed by the enemy I have learned to write down the thoughts that I am being offered, the ones I have been thinking. As I put them on paper and look at them I find it much easier to identify the lies — they just seem to stick out when written down. Then I can reject those lies and write down God's truth so that my mind can be renewed.

Sometimes when I am journaling God begins to speak words that I record just as He says them. His words can be affirming, they may be instructional, they may bring new revelation, or they may bring conviction of sin requiring repentance.

Sometimes I journal prayers to God — things my heart desires or my sorrow over some sin, my confession and repentance and thankfulness for His forgiveness.

"Sometimes I will journal if I am in a deep season of suffering and sadness. Daily as I cry out to Him, I know that in my current state of mind, I may forget things, or not be able to focus or concentrate, so it really aids me to write some things down. I am always amazed (but shouldn't be) when weeks later I read my journal, and God's amazing grace jumps off the page at me. I am so thankful and immediately praise Him for His Presence and direction." ~ Colleen

There is no journaling formula, but it is helpful to understand that God often speaks as we write out our thoughts, fears, hopes, questions.

"Journaling is how I primarily learned how to hear God's voice. I would pour out my heart on paper; then internally I would hear God speaking His thoughts back to me. His speaking at those times was a continuous flow of His thoughts and I recorded the words just as I heard them." ~ Kimberly

John Eldredge explains when he does not receive a clear answer from God, he will write out his questions on a piece of paper, one at a time. This allows him to sit before God with a single question on his heart as he prays and listens specifically issue by issue. As he listens he sets aside everything else which might otherwise cloud his thoughts. He purposefully refrains from weighing all the facts in his mind because He is not trying to figure out the best answer, He is positioning himself to hear God's answer. Eldredge notes, "There is a difference."[7]

Even if you choose not to journal on a regular/daily basis it is very important to write down words God speaks to you as soon as you hear them. I have learned from experience that we think we will remember what God said, but the enemy rushes in to cause confusion and to steal the "seed." Therefore, make it a practice to write down what you hear. You will find it to be very helpful when at times in the future you want to "check" what was said.

One of my best examples of this occurred the first time I actually heard God speak to me — not from a song, or through another person, or even the Bible — He simply chose to speak to me. He told me to lead a Bible study in a prison. And He gave me the name of the prison I was to enter (Marion Correctional). I did not write it down (I didn't realize how important it would be that I did so). But here is how the enemy then worked to bring confusion: some weeks after I heard the instruction I found myself in a Prison Fellowship training class believing *that* was the way God would use to get me into the prison He chose. I learned two shocking things in that training class: 1) there were no Prison Fellowship volunteers in Marion Correctional and 2) Marion Correctional was a *men's* prison — I thought "surely God would not send me into a men's prison to teach!" So, I came home from the training and said to my husband and daughter, it must be "Marysville" that God said to go into because that's a women's prison. As I looked back on these events, I saw how God protected the integrity of what He spoke to me. On the very same day I heard God's voice, I shared it with both my daughter and my husband so they were able to act as a memory for me and insist that God said *"Marion"* not *"Marysville."* Lesson learned! And not forgotten! What God says doesn't always make "sense" to us and the enemy will always try to steal and distort what we heard.

The point is: It is important to write down exactly what you heard. Generally speaking, the sooner you write it down the more accurate you will be. I have heard others suggest you keep a pencil and paper beside your bed just in case you need to write something down in the middle of the night.

Now that our study is drawing to a close, I want to leave you with an important caution to this entire conversation about hearing God's voice. As Christ-followers we are called to follow *Him*, to be in relationship with *Him*, to seek *His* will. "Hearing God … is for those who are devoted to the glory of God and the advancement of His kingdom. It is for the disciple of Jesus Christ who has no higher preference than to be like him."[8]

We should never ever place more priority on hearing His voice than we place on our relationship with Him. If we focus our attention on truly following Him as His disciple for His glory, hearing His voice will unfold in a meaningful, natural and appropriate way. "May listening to [God] become more than an exciting anomaly. May it be a daily pleasure."[9]

ENDNOTES

CHAPTER 1: LAYING THE FOUNDATION

1   Deere, Jack, *Surprised By The Voice of God* (Zondervan 1996) p. 117

2   Blackaby and Blackaby, *Hearing God's Voice* (B & H Publishing Group 2002) Preface, p. x

3   Mark 12:14; Romans 2:11

4   Shirer, Priscilla, *Discerning The Voice of God: How to Recognize When God Speaks* (LifeWay Press 2006) DVD Session 2, The Holy Spirit, emphasis in original teaching; subject also covered in the 2017 update of this study Session 2, The Holy Spirit

5   Batterson, Mark, *Whisper* (RightNow Media 2018) Session 4, The Seven Languages, teaching based on Batterson's book, *Whisper: How to Hear the Voice of God* (Multnomah 2017)

6   Shirer, Priscilla, *Discerning The Voice of God: How to Recognize When God Speaks* (LifeWay Press 2006) DVD Session 2, The Holy Spirit

7   Shirer, Priscilla, *Hearing the Voice of God*, Going Beyond Ministries, September 9, 2016. Retrieved from https://www.youtube.com (last accessed July 31, 2021)

8   Shirer, Priscilla, *Discerning The Voice of God: How to Recognize When God Speaks* (LifeWay Press 2006) DVD Session 1, Anticipating the Voice of God, quoting A. W. Tozer

9   Blackaby and Blackaby, *Hearing God's Voice* (B & H Publishing Group 2002) p. 48

10 Keil and Delitzsch, *The Keil & Delitzsch Commentary on the Old Testament*, Habakkuk 2:1. Retrieved from *The Discovery Bible* software developed by Gary Hill, HELPS Ministries Inc.

11 Keener, Craig S., *The Gospel Of John: A Commentary*, Volume One (Hendrickson Publishers 2003) John 16:13, p. 1039

12 *Ephesians 5:19-20 Commentary*, PreceptAustin, citing Vincent, *M. R. Word Studies in the New Testament*. Retrieved from https://www.preceptaustin.org/ephesians_519-20 (last (accessed July 10, 2021)

13 Waltke, Bruce K., *The Book of Proverbs: Chapters 1-15* (Eerdmans 2004) Proverbs 3:32, p. 271

14 Hill, Gary, *The Discovery Bible*, HELPS Ministries, Inc., [H]5475 *sôd*, italics in original; see also: *NET Bible Notes*, translator's note 100, Proverbs 3:32

15 Longman and Garland, editors, *The Expositor's Bible Commentary: 5 Psalms*, Revised Edition (Zondervan 2008) Psalm 25:12-14, p. 269

16 Blackaby and Blackaby, *Hearing God's Voice* (B & H Publishing Group 2002) p. 52

17 Morris, Robert, Pastor, Gateway Church, Sermon Series: *Frequency: The Whispers of God*, quoting Dallas Willard

CHAPTER 2: THE NORM NOT THE EXCEPTION

1   Eldredge, John, *Walking With God* (Thomas Nelson 2008) p. 44

[2] Rodney Clapp author of *New Creation: A Primer on Living in the Time Between the Times* (Cascade Books 2018) pp. 8-26 identifies 6 stages of God's history with His creation:

1) creation; 2) fall/failure of humanity; 3) the call of Abraham/the election of Israel; 4) Jesus the promised Messiah who rehearsed Israel's story and gave it the proper ending; 5) the inaugurated Kingdom of God; and 6) the coming fullness of God's Kingdom.

[3] John 12:49

[4] Morris, Robert, Pastor, Gateway Church, Sermon Series: *Frequency: Tune In. Hear God.* I'm A Sheep

[5] Sheets, Dutch, *The Pleasure of His Company*, Day 27, Chapter 27: The Advantage, GiveHim15, June 3, 2021. Retrieved from https://www.givehim15.com; Hill, Gary, *The Discovery Bible*, HELPS Ministries, Inc., [G]4851 *symphérō*

[6] I do not know the original source of this reference. I have noticed it is a book title, McKee, Sheb, *GPS: God's Positioning System* (Next Century Publishing 2016). I have also noticed that it is repeated frequently in blogs and web articles.

[7] Deere, Jack, *Surprised By The Voice of God* (Zondervan 1996) pp. 53-54

[8] Deere, Jack, *Surprised By The Voice of God* (Zondervan 1996) pp. 54-56

[9] Deere, Jack, *Surprised By The Voice of God* (Zondervan 1996) pp. 60-63

[10] Shirer, Priscilla, *Discerning the Voice of God: How to Recognize When God Speaks* (LifeWay Press 2006) DVD Session 2, The Holy Spirit

[11] Shirer, Priscilla, *Discerning the Voice of God: How to Recognize When God Speaks* (LifeWay Press 2006) DVD Session 2, The Holy Spirit

12   Shirer, Priscilla, *Discerning the Voice of God: How to Recognize When God Speaks* (LifeWay Press 2006) DVD Session 2, The Holy Spirit

13   Keener, Craig S., *The Gospel Of John: A Commentary*, Volume One (Hendrickson Publishers 2003) John 10:3-6, p. 808

14   Blackaby and King, *Experiencing God: Knowing and Doing The Will of God* (B & H Publishers 2004) p. 50

15   Source unknown, I heard a portion of a sermon on the radio one morning and the pastor used this phrase to refer to small life changes.

16   Blackaby and King, *Experiencing God: Knowing and Doing The Will of God* (B & H Publishers 2004) p. 46

17   Sheets, Dutch, *My Wife Is Always Right*, April 29, 2021, Give-Him15. Retrieved from http://gh15database.com

18   Murray, Andrew, *Abide in Christ* (Christian Literature Crusade 1997) p. 110

19   Wright, Tom, *Matthew For Everyone*, Part 1 (Society for Promoting Christian Knowledge 2002) p. 136

20   Wright, Tom, *Matthew For Everyone*, Part 1 (Society for Promoting Christian Knowledge 2002) p. 136

21   Murray, Andrew, *Abide in Christ* (Christian Literature Crusade 1997) p. 110, italics in original

22   Murray, Andrew, *The Inner Life* (Whitaker House 1984) p. 55 as quoted in Blackaby and Blackaby, *Hearing God's Voice* (B & H Publishing Group 2002) p. 15

23   Blackaby and King, *Experiencing God: Knowing and Doing The Will of God* (LifeWay Press 2007, reprinted 2015) 13-Session Bible Study, Unit 3, pp. 51-67

24   Waltke, Bruce K., *The Book of Proverbs: Chapters 1-15* (Eerdmans 2004) Proverbs 3:32, p. 271

25   MacArthur, John, *The MacArthur Study Bible* (Thomas Nelson 2006) study note Psalm 100:3, p. 818

26   Scholar Craig Keener refers to this promised new heart as "the specific eschatological endowment of a heart for obedience." He credits John's gospel for making clear that "this new nature comes 'from above,' 'from heaven,' but only through faith ([John] 3:15-16) in the Son who came from heaven (John 3:13) and was lifted there again by way of the cross (John 3:14)." Keener, Craig S., *The Gospel Of John: A Commentary*, Volume One (Hendrickson Publishers 2003) John 3:6, p. 554. Note: in the days in which the gospels were written it was widely believed that your origin affected your identity — therefore when John stresses a new birth from "above" he makes clear to his readers that this new birth gives them a new identity in Christ! Ibid., pp. 554-556

27   Waltke, Bruce K., *The Book of Proverbs: Chapters 1-15* (Eerdmans 2004) Proverbs 3:6, p. 244

CHAPTER 3: COMMON WAYS GOD SPEAKS

1   Batterson, Mark, *Whisper* (RightNow Media 2018) Session 4, The Seven Languages, teaching based on Batterson's book, *Whisper: How to Hear the Voice of God* (Multnomah 2017)

2   Deere, Jack, *Surprised By The Voice of God* (Zondervan 1996) p. 68, italics in original

3   Priscilla Shirer refers to the voice of God as His authoritative, self-authenticating voice. Priscilla Shirer, *Discerning the Voice of God: How to Recognize When God Speaks* (LifeWay Press 2006) DVD Session 2, The Holy Spirit

4   Batterson, Mark, *Whisper* (RightNow Media 2018) Session 1, The Power of a Whisper, teaching based on Batterson's book, *Whisper: How to Hear the Voice of God* (Multnomah 2017)

5   Batterson, Mark, *Chase the Lion: If Your Dream Doesn't Scare You, It's Too Small* (Multnomah 2016) pp. 78, 79

6   *Dictionary.com* entry for *speak*. Retrieved from https://www.
     dictionary.com/browse/speak, italics added (last accessed De-
     cember 7, 2022)

7   Blackaby and Blackaby, *Hearing God's Voice* (B & H Publishing
     Group 2002) p. 18, italics in original

8   Deere, Jack, *Surprised By The Voice of God* (Zondervan 1996)
     p. 112. Deere acknowledges "There are legitimate exceptions
     to this statement. There have been times in history, for var-
     ious reasons, when it has been impossible for the ordinary
     Christian to read the Bible on a regular basis. Where modern
     governments have banned the Bible, God seems to speak all
     the more to his children in dreams, visions, impressions, and
     other ways." Ibid., p. 367, Chapter 7, endnote 7

9   Lotz, Anne Graham, *Going Deeper in God's Word: A Bible
     Study from Anne Graham Lotz*, Decision Magazine, Sep-
     tember 8, 2017. Retrieved from https://billygraham.org/
     decision-magazine/september-2017/going-deeper-in-gods-
     word-a-bible-study-from-anne-graham-lotz/. Original source
     no longer available, however the same information can be
     found at: Lotz, Anne Graham, *Going Deeper in God's Word: A
     Summer Bible Study to Share*, July 24, 2019. Retrieved from
     https://billygraham.org.uk/p/going-deeper-in-gods-word-a-
     summer-bible-study-to-share/ (last accessed January 14, 2022)

10   "Biblical submission is placing yourself under the authority
     of God's Word by choice. It is a choice made willingly from
     the heart and with a happy spirit." Idleman, Kyle, *The Book
     of 1 Peter*, Session 3, 1 Peter 2:13-25. Retrieved from https://
     www.rightnowmedia.org (last accessed January 14, 2022)

11   Keener, Craig S., *Listening for God's Voice and Heart in Scrip-
     ture, A conversation with Craig S. Keener*, The Pneuma Review,
     February 9, 2017. Retrieved from PneumaReview.com /
     listening-for-gods-voice-and-heart-in-scripture-a-conversa-
     tion-with-craig-s-keener/ (last accessed July 11, 2021)

12 Lotz, Anne Graham, *Expecting to See Jesus: A Wake-Up Call for God's People* (Zondervan 2011) Scripture-Study Worksheet Instructions

13 Batterson, Mark, *Chase the Lion: If Your Dream Doesn't Scare You, It's Too Small* (Multnomah 2016) p. 122, italics in original

14 Personal Journal April 24, 2014

15 1 Corinthians 2:11-12

16 Deere, Jack, *Surprised By The Voice of God* (Zondervan 1996) p. 107

17 Deere, Jack, *Surprised By The Voice of God* (Zondervan 1996) p. 266, citing 1 Corinthians 8:1

18 Lotz, Anne Graham, *The Daniel Prayer: Prayer That Moves Heaven and Changes Nations* (Zondervan 2016) pp. 53,55

19 Shirer, Priscilla, *Hearing the Voice of God*, Going Beyond Ministries, September 9, 2016. Retrieved from https://www.youtube.com/watch?v=Ewi2iTi3Ec8 (last accessed July 31, 2021); Shirer, Priscilla, He Speaks To Me Preparing To Hear From God (LifeWay Press 2005, 2009) DVD#2, Summary

20 Shirer, Priscilla, *Hearing the Voice of God*, Going Beyond Ministries, September 9, 2016. Retrieved from https://www.youtube.com/watch?v=Ewi2iTi3Ec8 (last accessed July 31, 2021)

21 Deere, Jack, *Surprised By The Voice of God* (Zondervan 1996) p. 108

22 At times in this study I will refer to "the Holy Spirit" (His title) simply as "Holy Spirit" (His name). Because some might find that objectionable, let me explain. It is noteworthy that in the original Greek of John 20:22, for example, the phrase "*pneuma hagion*" (translated Holy Spirit) could properly be a name or a title, depending on how one reads the Greek. Similarly, we find in Scripture references to "Jesus" as His name, while "Christ" (Messiah) is His title. We alternate between name and title often in the English language. For example, we say,

"When Lincoln was the president" or "President Lincoln." If we are thinking of Holy Spirit as a name, it is already definite without the use of "'the" because a name does not need to be preceded by a definite article. I suggest discomfort with a reference to "Holy Spirit" may be our lack of familiarity with using His name. However, using His name rather than His title emphasizes the personal nature of the Holy Spirit. And that's my point.

23 Meyer, Joyce, *Hotline to Heaven*, Joyce Meyer Ministries. Retrieved from https://www.bing.com/videos/search?q=joyce+meyer+hotline+to+heaven&docid=608045082934340356&mid=243A0E-C2FBA3D41DEDA5243A0EC2FBA3D-41DEDA5&view=detail&FORM=VIRE (last accessed July 31, 2021)

24 Meyer, Joyce, *Hotline to Heaven*, Joyce Meyer Ministries. Retrieved from https://www.bing .com/videos/search?q=joyce+meyer+hotline+to+heaven&docid=608045082934340356&mid=243A0E-C2FBA3D41DEDA5243A0EC2FBA3D-41DEDA5&view=detail&FORM=VIRE (last accessed July 31, 2021)

25 Meyer, Joyce, Enjoying Everyday Life, 2017 interview with Priscilla Shirer re: Discerning the Voice of God. Retrieved from https://www.youtube.com/watch?v=s_LUYLhIx3Y&index=39&list=PLIU4-tWzKSoqtvp7rbNKu3IPtYw1OEK-C (last attempt to access July 13, 2021, video no longer available)

26 Warren, Rick, *What is Blocking God's Voice*, LightSource.com, 06/18/17. Retrieved from www.lightsource.com/ministry/daily-hope /what-is-blocking-gods-voice-hearing-the-voice-of-god-492758.html?ref=sc (last accessed July 11, 2021)

27 Acts 7:51

28 Hill, Gary, *The Discovery Bible*, HELPS Ministries, Inc., [G]496 *antipíptō*

29 Hill, Gary, *The Discovery Bible*, HELPS Ministries, Inc., Cognate: [G]3076 *lypéō*

30 Renner, Rick, *Sparkling Gems from the Greek* (Harrison House Publishers 2003) January 5, p. 9, italics in original

31 Renner, Rick, *Sparkling Gems from the Greek* (Harrison House Publishers 2003) January 5, p. 9

32 Hill, Gary, *The Discovery Bible*, HELPS Ministries, Inc., explanation of *Negated Greek Present Imperative*

33 Zodhiates, Spiros, *The Complete Word Study Dictionary: New Testament* (AMG Publishers 1992) word #4570 *sbennumi*, p. 1282

34 Hill, Gary, *The Discovery Bible*, HELPS Ministries Inc., explanation of *Negated Greek Present Imperative*

35 Kendall, R. T., *Holy Fire: A Balanced, Biblical Look At The Holy Spirit's Work in Our Lives* (Charisma House 2014) p. 20

36 Shirer, Priscilla, *Discerning God's Voice: How to Recognize When God Speaks* (LifeWay Press 2017) story told in older version of study

37 Keck, Leander E., *Romans*, Abingdon New Testament Commentaries (Abingdon Press 2005) Romans 8:1-17, p. 202

38 Keck, Leander E., *Romans*, Abingdon New Testament Commentaries (Abingdon Press 2005) Romans 8:1-17, p. 201

39 Kendall, R. T., *Total Forgiveness: Revised and Updated* (Charisma House 2002, 2007) Introduction, p. 11

40 I am intentionally repurposing the word "represent" by making a clear separation between the prefix "re" and the remainder of the word "present." The prefix "re" indicates repetition and has an ordinary meaning of "again" or "back." My goal in showing the word in this unique form is to highlight the truth that one who is God's representative does not act on his own accord, that representative is actually commissioned by God to "repeat" what God has done, to show "again" who God is.

CHAPTER 4: MORE COMMON WAYS GOD SPEAKS

[1]   See for example: Genesis 15:12; 46:2; Daniel 2:1,19; Matthew 2:12; 27:19; Acts 16:9-10

[2]   Blackaby and Blackaby, *Hearing God's Voice* (B & H Publishing Group 2002) p. 50

[3]   Virkler, Mark, *Hear God Through Your Dreams*, Session 2, The Principles of Dream Interpretation-1. This information is available at "Hear God Through Your Dreams," pp. 82-83 (cwgministries.org). Retrieved from http://objects.cwgministries.org/free/Hear%20God%20Through%20Your%20Dreams%20-%20Pages%2082-83.pdf (last accessed January 14, 2022). In 2016 Dr. Vickler's teaching appears to have been incorporated into a book he co-authored with his daughter, Charity Virkler Kayembe, entitled, *Hearing God Through Your Dreams Understanding The Language God Speaks At Night* (Destiny Image Publishers 2016)

[4]   Examples are: *Experiencing God* by Henry Blackaby and numerous studies by Priscilla Shirer, Jennifer Rothschild, and Beth Moore

[5]   Waltke, Bruce K., *The Book of Proverbs: Chapters 1-15* (Eerdmans 2004) Proverbs 12:15, Waltke translation, p. 517

[6]   Waltke, Bruce K., *The Book of Proverbs: Chapters 1-15* (Eerdmans 2004) Proverbs 11:14, Waltke translation, p. 490

[7]   Blackaby and Blackaby, *Hearing God's Voice* (B & H Publishing Group 2002) p. 161

[8]   For more information on what Bruce Wilkinson calls "border bullies" see Wilkinson, Bruce, *The Dream Giver* (Multnomah Publishers 2003) pp. 27-33; 100-111

[9]   Wilkinson, Bruce, *The Dream Giver* (Multnomah Publishers 2003) p.101

10 For more information on "border buddies" and "border busters" see Wilkinson, Bruce, *The Dream Giver* (Multnomah Publishers 2003) pp. 105-106

11 Morris, Robert, *Frequency Tune In. Hear God.* (W Publishing Group 2016) p. 112

12 Morris, Robert, *Frequency Tune In. Hear God.* (W Publishing Group 2016) p. 112

13 Longman and Garland, editors, *The Expositor's Bible Commentary: 5 Psalms*, Revised Edition (Zondervan 2008) Psalm 150 Overview, p. 1008, citing Brueggemann (*The Message of the Psalms*, 167), italics in original

14 Ezekiel 43:2; Revelation 1:15; 14:2

15 Balmer, Mark, Sermon: *Christ Followers Empowered by the Holy Spirit to Expand the Kingdom of God*, Acts 1, May 16, 2021, Calvary Chapel Melbourne

16 Hebrews 13:20

17 *Peace-Eirene (Greek Word Study)*, PreceptAustin. Retrieved from https://www.preceptaustin.org/peace_eirene (last accessed July 10, 2021)

18 Renner, Rick, *Sparkling Gems from the Greek* (Harrison House Publishers 2003) July 24, p. 529, italics in original

19 Hill, Gary, *The Discovery Bible*, HELPS Ministries, Inc., [G]1515 *eirēnē*

20 Hill, Gary, *The Discovery Bible*, HELPS Ministries, Inc., [G]5432 *phrouréō*

21 Hill, Gary, *The Discovery Bible*, HELPS Ministries, Inc., Cognate: [G]1018 *brabeúō*, citing E. Stauffer, TDNT 1.637-638

22 Hill, Gary, *The Discovery Bible*, HELPS Ministries, Inc., Cognate: [G]1018 *brabeúō*

23 Hill, Gary, *The Discovery Bible*, HELPS Ministries, Inc., Cognate: [G]1018 *brabeúō*, italics in original

24   Morris, Robert, *Frequency Tune In. Hear God.* (W Publishing Group 2016) pp. 113,122

25   Shirer, Priscilla, *Discerning the Voice of God: How To Recognize When God Speaks* (LifeWay Press 2017) Viewer Guide, Week Two, p. 39

26   Keener, Craig S., *The Gospel Of John: A Commentary*, Volume One (Hendrickson Publishers 2003) Introduction, p. 327

27   Lewis, C. S., *Miracles: A Preliminary Study* (Robert MacLehose and Company 1947) p. 11. Retrieved from https://archive.org/details/in.ernet.dli.2015.260876/page/nl/mode/2up (last accessed July 31, 2021)

28   "If anything extraordinary seems to have happened, we can always say that we have been the victims of an illusion. If we hold a philosophy which excludes the supernatural, this is what we always shall say." Lewis, C. S., *Miracles: A Preliminary Study* (Robert MacLehose and Company 1947) p. 11. Retrieved from https://archive.org/details/in.ernet.dli.2015.260876/page/nl/mode/2up (last accessed July 31, 2021)

29   Farrel, Pam, *A Woman God Can Use: Finding Your Place In His Plan* (Harvest House 1999) pp. 161-163

30   Blackaby and Blackaby, *Hearing God's Voice* (B & H Publishing Group 2002) p. 128

31   Deere, Jack, *Surprised By The Voice of God* (Zondervan 1996) p. 116

CHAPTER 5: FOUR IMPORTANT PRINCIPLES

1   Willard, Dallas, *Hearing God: Developing a Conversational Relationship with God*, Session 1, You Were Created for Intimate Friendship with God, based on Willard's book by same title (IVP Books 1984, 1993, 1999, 2012). Teaching retrieved from RightNow Media (last accessed January 14, 2022)

2   The common practice among near eastern shepherds is to be constantly talking with their flock as they lead them to find

pasture and water. In this way, the sheep become very familiar with their own shepherd's voice.

3   Keener, Craig S., *The Gospel Of John: A Commentary*, Volume One (Hendrickson Publishers 2003) John 10:3-6, p. 806

4   Keener, Craig S., *The Gospel Of John: A Commentary*, Volume One (Hendrickson Publishers 2003) John 10:1-10, p. 801

5   Keller, Phillip, *A Shepherd Looks At Psalm 23: An Inspiring And Insightful Guide To One Of The Best-Loved Bible Passages* (Zondervan 1970) p. 15

6   Based on my observation as my husband and I were on a tour bus traveling through the Jordanian countryside and observed fields with sheep and goats. Following my own observation, I noted that Craig Keener's commentary on the Gospel of John confirms what I observed by pointing out that sheep naturally "remain near the rest of the flock." Keener, Craig S., *The Gospel Of John A Commentary*, Volume One (Hendrickson Publishers 2003) John 10:1-10, p. 801

7   Renner, Rick, *Sparkling Gems from the Greek Volume II* (Harrison House Publishers 2016) March 28, p. 310, italics in original

8   Zodhiates, Spiros, *The Complete Word Study Dictionary: New Testament* (AMG Publishers 1992) entry for #1492 *eido*, p. 509

9   *2 Peter 1:12-21 Commentary*, PreceptAustin. Retrieved from http://www.preceptaustin.org/2_peter_112-21 (last accessed July 11, 2021)

10   Keener, Craig S., *The Gospel Of John: A Commentary*, Volume One (Hendrickson Publishers 2003) John 10:3-6, p. 808

11   Keener, Craig S., *The Gospel Of John: A Commentary*, Volume One (Hendrickson Publishers 2003) John 10:3-6, p. 808, italics added

12   Mounce, William D., editor, *Complete Expository Dictionary of Old & New Testament Words* (Zondervan 2006) entry for *know*, p. 383

13   Henry Blackaby's study *Experiencing God: Knowing and Doing The Will of God* is probably one of the best studies I know of to help us understand we were created for relationship with God.

14   Deere, Jack, *Surprised By The Power Of The Spirit: Discovering How God Speaks and Heals Today* (Zondervan 1993) p. 265

15   Eldredge, John, *Walking With God* (Thomas Nelson 2008) p. 201

16   Blackaby and Blackaby, *Hearing God's Voice* (B & H Publishing Group 2002) p. 214

17   Hill, Gary, *The Discovery Bible*, HELPS Ministries, Inc., [H]8085 *šāma'*

18   Waltke, Bruce K., *The Book of Proverbs: Chapters 1-15* (Eerdmans 2004) Proverbs 1:5, p. 179

19   Balmer, Mark, Sermon: *Know the Benefits of the Holy Spirit Who Lives in Every Christ Follower*, May 2, 2021, Calvary Chapel Melbourne

20   Eldredge, John, *Walking With God* (Thomas Nelson 2008) p. 123

21   Eldredge, John, *Walking With God* (Thomas Nelson 2008) p. 123

22   Blackaby and Blackaby, *Hearing God's Voice* (B & H Publishing Group 2002) p. 150

23   Zodhiates, Spiros, *The Complete Word Study Dictionary: New Testament* (AMG Publishers 1992) word #2309, p. 727

24   MacArthur, John, *The MacArthur Study Bible* (Thomas Nelson 2006) study note Philippians 2:13 to will and to work, p. 1793

25 *Holman Christian Standard Bible*, Study Bible edition (Holman Bible Publishers 2010) study note Philippians 2:12-13, p. 2046

26 MacArthur, John, *The MacArthur Study Bible* (Thomas Nelson 2006) study note Philippians 2:13 to will and to work, p. 1793, italics added, citation omitted

27 *Philippians 2:13 Commentary*, Precept Austin, citing F. F. Bruce. Retrieved from https://www.preceptaustin.org/philippians_213 (last accessed January 11, 2022)

28 Batterson, Mark, *Whisper* (RightNow Media 2018) Session 2, The Whispering Spot, teaching based on Batterson's book, *Whisper: How to Hear the Voice of God* (Multnomah 2017)

29 Shirer, Priscilla, *Discerning The Voice of God: How to Recognize When God Speaks* (LifeWay Press 2017) story told in older version of study

30 Deere, Jack, *Surprised By The Voice of God* (Zondervan 1996) p. 310

31 Deere, Jack, *Surprised By The Voice of God* (Zondervan 1996) p. 310-311

32 Lysa TerKeurst describes her first-thing-when-she-wakes-up communication with God as "exchanging whispers with God before [she begins to exchange] the shouts of the world." Lysa Terkeurst, *Is God Speaking To Me?* interview by Joni Lamb, Joni Table Talk, Daystar TV, April 26, 2021, replay www.bing.com (last accessed May 22, 2021)

CHAPTER 6: FOUR MORE IMPORTANT PRINCIPLES

1 *Horse Body Language: How To Read It And Understand It - The Horse Owner's Resource* (Equusmagazine.com). Retrieved from https://equusmagazine.com/behavior/horse-body-language (last accessed July 13, 2021)

2 Parker, Richard, *Why Do My Cat's Ears Keep Twitching?* (SeniorCatWellness.com). Retrieved from https://www.senior-

catwellness.com/cats-ears-keep-twitching (last accessed July 10, 2021). Of note is that the article points out cats are able to hear sounds 1.6 octaves above humans.

3   *Our animal inheritance: Humans perk up their ears, too, when they hear interesting sounds,* Saarland University, ScienceDaily. ScienceDaily, 7 July 2020. Retrieved from www.sciencedaily. com/releases/2020/07/200707113337.htm (last accessed July 11, 2021)

4   *Brown-Driver-Briggs Hebrew and English Lexicon,* Unabridged, Electronic Database, entry for [H]7181. *qashab.* Copyright © 2002, 2003, 2006 by Biblesoft, Inc. All rights reserved. Used by permission. BibleSoft.com. Retrieved from https://www. biblehub.com/Hebrew/7181.htm

5   See for example: Psalm 5:2; 10:17; 17:1; 55:2; 142:6

6   Baker and Carpenter, *The Complete WordStudy Dictionary of the Old Testament* (AMG Publishers 2003) entry for #7181 *qasab,* p. 1018

7   *Merriam-Webster.com Dictionary,* Merriam-Webster, entry for *Hearken.* Retrieved from https://www.merriam-webster.com/ dictionary/hearken (last accessed May 22, 2021)

8   Source: Robert D. Pace, originally PulpitToday.org; now RevelationCentral.com. Original retrieval site https://robertdpace. com/how-to-hear-gods-voice. The original source site no longer exists on the internet. As of May 23, 2021, the Sermon titled: *How To Hear God's Voice* from which this quote was taken can be found at https://revelationcentral.com/how-to-hear-gods-voice. Pace received his degree in Biblical Historical Studies from Lee University in 1977 and is an international speaker.

9   Hill, Gary, *The Discovery Bible,* HELPS Ministries, Inc., [G]498 *antitássomai,* italics in original

10 Wagner, C. Peter, *Humility* (Regal Books 2002) pp. 51-52

11 Wagner, C. Peter, *Humility* (Regal Books 2002) p. 52

12   Wagner, C. Peter, *Humility* (Regal Books 2002) p. 53. Wagner credits Eddie Hyatt for his research which answered the question. Hyatt's research provided some details about how the dangerous slide from humility to pride unfolded. Ibid, pp. 52-53

13   Wagner, C. Peter, *Humility* (Regal Books 2002) pp. 22-23. Peter Wagner points out that in Paul's list of fruit of the Spirit (Galatians 5:22-23) the word "gentleness" or in some translations "meekness" is the Greek word *prayotes* {prah-oo'-tace} which is one of the two New Testament root words for humility. Wagner writes, "It is, therefore, important to understand that humility is a fruit of the Spirit. If we stay filled with the Holy Spirit, more than likely we will stay humble." *The Theological Dictionary of the New Testament* indicates that the root Greek word *praus* is found 12 times in the Greek translation of the Old Testament (LXX) for various Hebrew words primarily relating to the social position of a servant or inferior person and thus carries the nuance of humbleness. Bromiley, Geoffrey W., *Theological Dictionary of the New Testament*, Abridged in One Volume (Eerdmans 1985) entry for *praus*, p. 930

14   Journal Entry July 2, 2017 with addendums

15   Genesis 37:2 specifically says Joseph was 17 when he brought a bad report to his father about his brothers. The reader can assume that the remaining events of Chapter 37 (including the dream he had about his brothers bowing down to him) would have taken place about the same time.

CHAPTER 7: GOD'S VOICE

1   See for example: Matthew 11:15, Mark 4:9; Revelation 2:7, 11, 17, 29; 3:3, 13, 20, 22. Scholar Grant Osborne notes that there is "a strong emphasis on the responsibility of God's people to open their ears." He points out that the phrase "Let the one who has an ear to hear, listen" could be translated as "'Let the one who is willing to hear, listen." He then concludes

by reminding his readers that "throughout both testaments, 'to hear' is 'to obey.'" Osborne, Grant, *Revelation* (Baker Academic 2002) Revelation 2:7a, p. 121, italics added

2   Sheets, Dutch, *The Pleasure of His Company*, Day 5, Chapter 5: The Search, GiveHim15, May 11, 2021. Retrieved from http://gh15database.com

3   Batterson, Mark, *Whisper* (RightNow Media 2018) Session 4, The Seven Languages, teaching based on Batterson's book, *Whisper: How to Hear the Voice of God* (Multnomah 2017)

4   Deere, Jack, *Surprised By The Voice of God* (Zondervan 1996) p. 175

5   Pete Briscoe, Senior Pastor of Bent Tree Bible Fellowship, refers to these two voices as the leading voice and the misleading voice. Briscoe, Pete, *Hearing the Holy Spirit's Voice*, Session 2, Listening to the Voice Inside (Telling the Truth 2015). Retrieved from https://www.rightnowmedia.org (last accessed January 14, 2022)

6   Harris, Archer and Waltke, editors, *Theological Wordbook of the Old Testament* (Moody Press 1999) word #848c, p. 366

7   Harris, Archer and Waltke, editors, *Theological Wordbook of the Old Testament* (Moody Press 1999) word #848c, p. 366

8   Morris, Robert, Pastor, Gateway Church, Sermon Series: *Frequency: Tune In. Hear God.*

9   In Romans 7-8, for example, Paul contrasts "two kinds of persons — those who exist 'according to the flesh' and those who exist 'according to the Spirit;'" the flesh and the Spirit are two "sovereignties that govern one's life." Keck, Leander E., *Romans*, Abingdon New Testament Commentaries (Abingdon Press 2005) Romans 8:1-17, pp. 201-202. Paul was not alone in identifying only two sources of action, ancient Jewish scrolls found in the caves at Qumran contained writings which "attributes all actions to either the spirit of truth or the spirit of leading astray." Keener, Craig S., *The Gospel Of John:*

A Commentary, Volume One (Hendrickson Publishers 2003) John 3:6, p. 554, footnote 203

10 *Discovery of "Thought Worms" Opens Window to the Mind*, Neuroscience News, July 14, 2020. Retrieved from https://neurosciencenews.com/thought-worms-16639 (last accessed July 11, 2021)

11 Assuming 16 hours of wake time per day

12 Adapted from the book *A Woman God Can Use: Finding Your Place In His Plan* by Pam Farrel (Harvest House 1999) pp. 161-163, amended to incorporate the counsel of a variety of other Christian leaders and many of my own experiences

13 Zodhiates, Spiros, *The Complete Word Study Dictionary: New Testament* (AMG Publishers 1992) word #225, p. 120

14 Keener, Craig S., *The IVP Bible Background Commentary: New Testament* (Intervarsity Press 1993) John 14:17, p. 300

15 *Reticular Activating System: Definition & Function*, Study.com. Retrieved from https://study.com/academy/lesson/reticular-activating-system-definition-function.html (last accessed July 31, 2021). While the author of this study material attributed the RAS to evolution, the truth is that God designed our bodies including the way in which our brain functions.

16 I am indebted to Lance Wallnau for his short teaching about our reticular activator when he was speaking at Oasis in Middletown, Ohio on May 23, 2021. I had observed this phenonium in my own life but did not understand why it worked as it did until I heard Lance teach on what he called a "part of the mysterious design between your spirit and your soul." It was one of those *aha* moments.

17 Warren, Rick, *Obedience Leads to Peace*, Daily Hope with Rick Warren, April 10, 2018. Retrieved from https://www.crosswalk.com/devotionals/daily-hope-with-rick-warren/daily-hope-with-rick-warren-april-10-2018.html (last accessed July 11, 2021)

18   The fact that God disciplines us so we can enjoy His fellowship and blessings is proof of His love. C. S. Lewis has concluded that when we complain about discipline which might include suffering we're not asking for *more* love, we're actually asking God to love us *less*! Waltke, Bruce K., *The Book of Proverbs: Chapters 1-15* (Eerdmans 2004) Proverbs 3:12, p. 250, citing C. S. Lewis, *The Problem of Pain* (Geoffrey Bles and Centenary 1940) pp. 30-33

19   Stanley, Charles, *How To Listen To God* (Thomas Nelson 1985) p. 19

20   Longman and Garland, editors, *The Expositor's Bible Commentary: 5 Psalms*, Revised Edition (Zondervan 2008) Reflections: The Praise of Yahweh, p. 505

CHAPTER 8: SATAN'S VOICE

1   *Spirit Filled Life Bible* (Thomas Nelson 1991), Word Wealth Matthew 11:6 offended. *skandalizo*, p. 1424

2   Personal Journal April 28, 2021. I do not recall ever hearing the phrase "scout thought" or seeing it in any of the books I have read on hearing God's voice. The phrase was brought to my mind by Holy Spirit on April 28, 2021 in a season when I was editing this study. Interestingly as soon as I heard the words in my spirit I knew exactly what they referred to and understood this truth was to be added to the study.

3   Ezekiel 28:13; Isaiah 14:12-15

4   Keener, Craig S., *The Gospel Of John: A Commentary*, Volume One (Hendrickson Publishers 2003) John 10:3-6, p. 808

5   Sheets, Dutch, *The Pleasure of His Company*, Day 25, Chapter 25: The Look, GiveHim15, June 1, 2021. Retrieved from http://gh15database.com

6   1 Samuel 15:23 NLT

7   Zodhiates, Spiros, *The Complete Word Study Dictionary: New Testament* (AMG Publishers 1992) entry for #2723, *kategoreo*, p. 850

8   Zodhiates, Spiros, *The Complete Word Study Dictionary: New Testament* (AMG Publishers 1992) entry for #2725, *kategoros*, p. 850

9   The Greek word *katakrima* {kat-ak'-ree-mah}, like the word "accuser" *kategoros* {kat-ay'-gor-os}, was used commonly in a legal context. Bromiley, Geoffrey W., *Theological Dictionary of the New Testament*, Abridged in One Volume (Eerdmans 1985) entry for *krino* (*katakrima*), p. 469

10   Bromiley, Geoffrey W., *Theological Dictionary of the New Testament*, Abridged in One Volume (Eerdmans 1985) entry for *katakrino, katakrima, katakrisis*, p. 475

11   Personal Journal May 28, 2021 as I was in my own battle with conviction versus condemnation

12   Kendall, R. T., *Total Forgiveness: Revised and Updated* (Charisma House 2002, 2007) p. 161

13   *Oxford English and Spanish Dictionary, Synonyms, and Spanish to English Translator*, entry for *shame*. Retrieved from https://www.lexico.com/en/definition/shame (last accessed July 11, 2021)

14   Bolton, Jane, Psy.D., M.F.T., *What We Get Wrong About Shame, Why is shame such a painful emotion?* Psychology Today, May 18, 2009, quoting Gershen Kaufman, contemporary scholar on shame. Retrieved from https://www.psychologytoday.com/us/blog/your-zesty-self/200905/what-we-get-wrong-about-shame (last accessed July 11, 2021)

15   Lamia, Mary C., Ph.D., Clinical Psychologist, *Shame: A Concealed, Contagious, and Dangerous Emotion*, Psychology Today, April 4, 2011. Retrieved from https://www.psychologytoday.com/us/blog/intense-emotions-and-strong-feelings/201104/

shame-concealed-contagious-and-dangerous-emotion (last accessed July 11, 2021)

16   Arnold, Clinton E., general editor., *Zondervan Illustrated Bible Backgrounds Commentary*, Vol. 4 (Zondervan 2002) Hebrews 12:2, p. 75

17   Hill, Gary, *The Discovery Bible*, HELPS Ministries, Inc., [G]2706 *kataphroneō*

18   Rothschild, *Jennifer, Psalm 23: The Shepherd With Me*, Participant Workbook (LifeWay Press 2018, 2020) p. 179

19   Keesee, Drenda, *Shark Proof: How To Deal with Difficult People* (Free Indeed Publishers 2018) p. 50

20   Moore, Beth, *So Long Insecurity* (Tyndale House Publishers 2010)

CHAPTER 9: ADDITIONAL INSIGHTS INTO GOD'S VOICE

1   Heiser, Michael S., *The Unseen Realm: Recovering the Supernatural Worldview of the Bible* (Lexham Press 2015) p. 64

2   A worship leader at Calvary Chapel Melbourne shared a testimony with this instruction, "When we can't understand what God is doing in the present, rehearse the truth we already know about Him from the past." The worship leader credited the teaching of Chuck Smith, founder Calvary Chapel, for this wisdom.

3   Smith, Chuck, *Calvary Chapel Distinctives: The Foundational Principles of the Calvary Chapel* Movement (The Word For Today 2000, 11th printing 2019) p. 119

4   Morris, Robert, Sermon: *Value His Voice (Hearing God's Voice)*, *Frequency Sermon Series*, published on Aug 14, 2015, Gateway Church

5   Batterson, Mark, *Whisper* (RightNow Media 2018) Session 2, The Whispering Spot, teaching based on Batterson's book, *Whisper: How to Hear the Voice of God* (Multnomah 2017)

6   Eldredge, John, *Walking With God* (Thomas Nelson 2008) p. 75, italics in original

7   Eldredge, John, *Walking With God* (Thomas Nelson 2008) p. 143

8   Eldredge, John, *Walking With God* (Thomas Nelson 2008) p. 32, italics in original

9   Eldredge, John, *Walking With God* (Thomas Nelson 2008) pp. 31-32

10   Eldredge, John, *Walking With God* (Thomas Nelson 2008) p. 67

11   Eldredge, John, *Walking With God* (Thomas Nelson 2008) p. 81, italics in original

12   Merrill, Eugene H., editor, *The Bible Knowledge Word Study, The Gospels* (Victor 2002) Matthew 6:16, Fast (*nesteuete*), p. 59

CHAPTER 10: FINE TUNING

1   Meyer, Joyce, *Enjoying Everyday Life*, 2017 interview with Priscilla Shirer re: Discerning the Voice of God. Retrieved from https://www.youtube.com/watch?v=s_LUYLhIx3Y&in-dex=39&list=PLIU4-tWzKSoqtvp7rbNKu3IPtYw1OEK-C (last attempt to access July 13, 2021, video no longer available)

2   Italics in original

3   "I tested you at the waters of Meribah" (Psalm 81:7; cf. Deuteronomy 8:2,16). Rephidim (Exodus 17:1,8; 19:2) means rests or stays, i.e. resting places. From the murmuring about the lack of water the place was called "Massah" and "Meribah."

4   Shirer, Priscilla, *Discerning The Voice of God: How to Recognize When God Speaks* (LifeWay Press 2017) Week 2, The Holy Spirit, commenting on an interview she had with Henry Blackaby

5   Matthew 5:48

6   Merrill, Eugene H., editor, *The Bible Knowledge Word Study, The Gospels* (Victor 2002) Matthew 5:48, Perfect (*teleioi*), p. 57

7   Shirer, Priscilla, *Discerning The Voice of God: How to Recognize When God Speaks* (LifeWay Press 2017) Week 7, Speak Lord. See also; Mackey, Angela, *What My Heart Does, Rethinking My Thinking*, October 27, 2011. Retrieved from http://re-thinkingmythinking.info/2011/10/what-my-heart-does/ (last accessed July 31, 2021)

8   Shirer, Priscilla, *Discerning The Voice of God: How to Recognize When God Speaks* (LifeWay Press 2017) Week 2, The Holy Spirit, Participant Workbook, Day Three Checks and Balances, pp. 54-55

9   Wood, Shane T., Ph.D., *The Book of Acts*, lecture series, Ozark Christian College. Retrieved from https://www.shanejwood.com/the-book-of-acts/ (last accessed July 31, 2021)

10   Terkeurst, Lysa, *Is God Speaking To Me?* interview by Joni Lamb, Joni Table Talk, Daystar TV, April 26, 2021, replay www.bing.com (last accessed May 22, 2021)

11   "If we function according to our ability alone, we get the glory; if we function according to the power of the Spirit within us, God gets the glory." Kendall, R. T., *Holy Fire: A Balanced, Biblical Look At The Holy Spirit's Work in Our Lives* (Charisma House 2014) p. 128, quoting Henry Blackaby

12   Another filter Lysa Terkeurst says she uses to determine God's voice is whether the instruction she receives would please God. Lysa Terkeurst, *Is God Speaking To Me?* interview by Joni Lamb, Joni Table Talk, Daystar TV, April 26, 2021, replay www.bing.com (last accessed May 22, 2021)

CHAPTER 11: GROWING MORE CONFIDENT

1   Terkeurst, Lysa, *Is God Speaking To Me?* interview by Joni Lamb, Joni Table Talk, Daystar TV, April 26, 2021, replay www.bing.com (last accessed May 22, 2021)

2   Morris, Robert, Pastor, Gateway Church, *Frequency Sermon Series: Heed What You Hear*

3   Morris, Robert, Pastor, Gateway Church, Sermon series: *In His Presence.* The prefix omni means "all." God is all present. In His omnipresence God is simultaneously present at all times with all His fullness to every part of creation He is always available to us — we cannot flee from His omnipresence. Hank Hanegraff, *Explaining God's Omnipresence*, The Bible Answer Man, 8/5/2015. Retrieved from https://www.youtube.com/watch?v=KfsfupNwEoA (last accessed January 14, 2022). God's inner presence refers to Holy Spirit who is the unmediated presence of God as power that enables the Christ-follower to live in accord with God's perfect will. Keck, Leander E., *Romans,* Abingdon New Testament Commentaries (Abingdon Press 2005) Romans 8:1-17, p. 201

4   Actually, in those days, people thought their god was directly connected to the land where He ruled — so Jonah likely thought he was fleeing from God altogether —even His omnipresence.

5   Hill, Gary, *The Discovery Bible*, HELPS Ministries, Inc., [G]991 *blépō*

6   *2 Corinthians 4:18 Commentary*, Precept Austin. Retrieved from https://www.preceptaustin.org/2corinthians_418_commentary (last accessed July 31, 2021)

7   Eldredge, John, *Walking With God* (Thomas Nelson 2008) p. 202

8   Willard, Dallas, *Hearing God: Developing a Conversational Relationship with God* (IVP Books 1999) p. 70

9   Sheets, Dutch, *A Prophetic Dream of a Founding Father*, GiveHim15, April 26, 2021. Retrieved from http://gh15database.com/